BUY ME, GET ME FREE

Copyright © 2018 by Ariel Samuel Ackrum

All rights reserved.
No part of this publication may be reproduced, distributed, or transmitted in any form or by any means, including photocopying, recording, or other electronic or mechanical methods, without the prior written permission of the publisher, except in the case of brief quotations embodied in critical reviews and certain other noncommercial uses, such as research or private study, permitted by copyright law. For permission requests, email publisher at the address listed below.

Simulacradelic Press
Atlanta, GA
simulacradelicpress@gmail.com
www.simulacradelic.com

Cover & Design by Seth Stubbs
Edited by Seth Stubbs

Library of Congress Control Number: 2018930910
ISBN-13: 978-0-9993980-2-9 (PBK)
1. Poetry 2. Philosophy

First Edition

10 9 8 7 6 5 4 3 2 1

Printed in the United States of America

BUY ME, GET ME FREE

NEW POEMS

ARIEL SAMUEL ACKRUM

For all my friends. You all appeared in my life like a cart of popsicles in the desert. You couldn't sustain me, but you flavored the earth.

CONTENTS

Mass Merger   11

LumpedIn   95

January 2016   155

Mass Merger:
Volumetric Poetry without Contradictions

If I told you that there is nothing on *any of the channels herein* but more of the Same—*indeed, nothing useful—wouldn't you tune in anyway, hoping for an Accident?*

1. The war is one that, one-sided, cannot be fought

> In the war between one and many,
> you cannot choose the side of the one.
>
> The one is not a 'side'.
> Only the many is a 'side'.
>
> Fascists and democrats share manyness.
>
> Politics and business and economics and sex
> share manyness.
>
> Artistic movements and fun and search-engines
> share manyness.
>
> The one is the fire.
> The one is the god.
> The one is the dead-man.

Mass Merger

The one is no-one.

Create seminal works: many.
Incorporate the present: many.

Travel over intimacy: one.
Home-bodied over out-goer: one.

Only the many criticize how I live.
Only the many want me to contribute.
Only the many want me
to raise my hand to speak
and hang myself with an agreeable noose.
They are doing worse than pissing in your coffee.
They are filling your coffee with syrup
and making you say idiotic names
of idiotic foods and drinks.
Only the many want me to die quietly
with the lethal injection of shame.
Only the many wants to be exalted.

Your love is inferior to my love,
what could it add to me?

Your love is shame, wants shame.
Kill the social smokers,
the beer-chuggers,
the acceptance speech fawners,
the commencement speech givers.

Kill the bribers,
the tote-baggers like carpetbaggers,
the solidarity hashtaggers
as dismembered as hash-browns
but not as golden,
the flag-downers and the upholders.

My suicide is not a commitment.
They are all suicide *committers*.

Buy Me, Get Me Free

Just listen to David Foster Wallace's speech
about his own, self-made cognitive behavioral therapy.
He killed himself shortly after,
but you will forgive him for that.

These habitual self-loathers
that have perverted Nietzsche
and have called Baudrillard
a 'cultural critic and/or theorist'.

They are at home with nihilism
and yet complain over every social channel.

Luckily, in the space *I* inhabit,
which is not the Internet of their chatter,
I don't hear their screams.

Their joy exists only when measured,
only existing on a graph.
Their summits are as flat as their screens.
Their touch is as glass-eyed as their screens.
Their intelligence is as bright
and blue
and sleepless as their screens.

They can't sit still
without checking their own pulses on a monitor,
without checking the camera feeds
in their empty houses,
without their personalized policeman
firehosing them to their seats
or without tweeting about the oppressiveness
of their own glutei maximi.

They document the ounces of water they drink in a day.
They display their empty liquor bottles above the cabinets.
They interpret their own dreams,
and they have adulterated childhood
with playground guards,

Mass Merger

learning centers
and detail-oriented joy.

Their side is the only one you can *choose*—
and you still *want to choose a side*?

I am not a side.
If I could choose 'my side',
that's because there is no I to it at all, just a me.

2. de-ranged long range

How can I remember anything
when none of it is directly lived
and proceeds from representation,
always on call temporarily?

Signs and systems change like sluts
and can never be direct.
Many names are given to
the thing, which is singular.

The words either lead or follow
the general mood, reality,
which is coercive or complicit
to the feelings and the actions.

My love feels up the long-distance.
Focusing on what is lacking
will be something we agree on,
and that will make up for nothing.

I de-fertilize with porn.
The screen gives me a distance
the machine can't match in control,
a distance with which only trauma competes.

Buy Me, Get Me Free

I don't feel the love feelings
even when they have some context
because they are out of place.
The irrational is unreal, or whatever.

Now, my power without weights
will wallow in its discharge
like an orca's cooled back
venting happily in theatric cruelty.

3. Dis-Barrage (*French for disparage*)

My eyes 'focus' on the television,
but I lose it, myself and track of time
as time's *tracks*
that disappear horizontally
mark me.
I'm not ashamed because I'm not true.

Everything is alright,
nothing is better,
but everything is the twin of nothing,
'competing' in a duopoly—
neither affecting the other's business.
I don't think about anything
but the showings listed
or the things on the home screen.

In there, there is no out there, no audacious strangeness—
and there, women are always involved,
for better or worse.

If you're out there God,
I'm sorry I'm "so fucking boring."
By all means, change the channel
and stop asking questions.
To young MTV bucks

Mass Merger

suffocating themselves
with an image they don't own but amplify,
or casino superstars
or even to local news anchors.

Haven't moved, or spoken, in 4 hours.
I suffer from a lack of mobility and employability.
It had to be this way.

Look down: hand in pants.
I think about writing, about being a writer.
I try not to think about the lack of meaning
generated by its expression;
however, communication is speech that's inexpressive
but inexpensive—
language being the most efficient,
free-floating mode of production.

This is it.
This is fucking it.
Haven't spoken to anyone in days
…uh oh, my neurons will fire even more slowly
and I'll be shored up like
the Alzheimer's old-timers.
The media want me to know that.
Behavioral patterns are too rigid
for our anthropo-scenic, *climatic* day-to-day.
It's never going to get better,
but it simultaneously can't get any worse.
Either way, who knows?

I can't watch the heroes win any more…
the smiles,
the miracles
or the deus ex machina.

I need a god's help
because I am too neutral to intervene—
even more neutral than God, fuck—

and if I can't seduce God,
I don't want to fucking play
because the hysterics have blackmailed me
into the dramatic simulation of seduction,

and now you're with the guy who'd
get bottom in the gangbang.

Don't look down.
Don't ever look down.

4. Fast food orgy

They all always seem to be circling one another,
jerking one another.
You never hear them talking ill of one another,
even though they all speak the same language,
because they don't talk much.
It's unnecessary.
The ads leave no room for misinterpretation.

You can really come and go as you please
in each
without affecting the sales
of the others.
You can enter them all if you want...
shit in one,
piss in another
and eat out a third.

There is no contradiction
in that commutation...

5. the genie's genus and our genius

>People have had their certainties.
>
>Socrates was sure that he knew nothing—
>he could prove it!
>
>Descartes was sure that there was God
>to turn the crystal into a mirror.
>
>Montaigne was sure he knew what was bad for him.
>
>If I'm to *have my doubt
>and my certainty too*,
>
>the only plausibility I offer
>is that there's more than a human lifespan's worth of media,
>
>more episodes than I will have had hours,
>
>more memes than I will have had memories,
>
>more information than I will have had thoughts—
>
>in short, the one thing I am almost certain of
>is that I have consumed more media
>than I have had experiences.
>
>Virtual space gives the impression
>of being greater than space
>and *outstripping magnetism*—
>and it has the eventual genius
>of creating a timescale in which it is always too early to tell
>if it is God.
>
>And I'm grateful for this—
>liberated from them in their extremes,
>having expelled them from their unapproachability.

6. The essential is essentially missing the inessential

When I was created, God left out all the essentials.
There is depth to me, if you are convinced,
but nothing fills it.
Like a mystical explanation, I am less than shallow.
If a mystical explanation
is anything like a mystical experience,
it destroys meaning.
God made me neither true nor false,
mostly just hokey pokey, folk psychology and graffiti—
but with love.

My world is too small
to not be today considered immoral.
The microscopy of my world is not the perfect counterpart
to the expansion of the world in its too-muchness.
The world, like evil, is a fractal
that renews its formula in every new eminence,
at every level or perspective,
with each new style of instrument
or approach.
That must be why Descartes found the evil genie
and started doing mathematical calculations.

I masturbated twice consecutively
to a random porn I didn't love or even like.
I approach 'real sex'
with 'real people'
basically the same way,
except I can't cum twice.

In the room I am in,
there are the couch that holds three retractable cushions,
two couch pillows and a laptop,
the coffee table—
on which sits an iPad,
the iPad's case/Bluetooth keyboard,
a paper towel roll,

a wallet with debit, credit, metro, I.D. cards in it,
a cell phone,
Ray-Ban sunglasses,
a remote control for the television,
an empty bottle and its plastic top,
a pack of cigarettes,
a laptop charger—
then the big screen television,
5 surround sound speakers,
two receivers,
inapproximable wires,
two chairs, an end table on which
there is a lamp and a drink coaster.

That's thirty-seven objects
including me,
and—because this is a poem—
I left out some things.
There are infinite sets of things
in this small room in which I am outnumbered
without including details or parts.

I miss you.
The calculations interrupt that.

7. The Deep South

Like a long dick that goes too deep
to hit the shallow g-spot,
you can be wrong about your own sadness.

The elderly are not weak, sad or dying.
They can mock your smooth skin
and your perfect teeth.
They can look up at you like a child
and eviscerate you with wonder.

The poor are not produced by scarcity.
Some of them do not watch the news
or read or go to school,
so they know not the language of their misfortune.
They look at their toothless skeletons in the mirror
and see New York models,
except that the models are uglier
because they need to be convinced of their beauty.

The flies, fire ants and gnats
worship your rotting, festering body
like a god of riches.

Here, death dreams of you,
wastes his riches on you
and invites you to his vacation home without a VIP section.

Here, death is your friend,
and he will even DP your girlfriend with you,
letting you get the asshole
if that is your flavor.

8. nostalgia buffet

The extrasensitive types
of the shaman, prophet, saint, poet and artist
are but the Mob Wives of reality
who assault it
by tearing out its extensions.

Their surgical trashiness
shows the revolutionary consciousness
as the husk of a Cicada.
Empty and transparent, gutted by worker ants,
but still visible.

The absurd excessiveness of existence

Mass Merger

can be seen in the huge fake titties of women
that swing like a dead body attached to a parachute,
tangled in a tree—

Everything is tongue in cheek,
but the tongues are only Airheads candies.

9. Signs according to demand

>   I thought God had ADHD toward me
>   and skimmed me, side-eye, like a magazine
>   in which sex advice columns spoke wisdom
>   that changed uselessly issue to issue.
>
>   I seek His attention negatively.
>   And I dare Him to react physically.
>   He seems absent-minded upon first glance
>   like introverts considered shy or rude.
>
>   The Father follows His whim and withdraws
>   His love like a polymorphous woman
>   caught up in the material aspect
>   of what is in or out, not what's worthwhile.
>
>   God, do you secretly love me, are you
>   scared of letting yourself go in Spirit—
>   no! you can't be closed off, transcendental!
>   Do I not affect you, absent lover?
>
>   Too wrapped up in my own, one mental life
>   that stretches itself between two directions
>   until it has lost elasticity
>   and drops flaccidly like an old, wet sock—
>
>   otherwise, it stays tight and stays rigid
>   like a body without some exercise
>   then becomes brittle like high-end cocaine

that shoots more quickly up to a blocked brain—

You will delete all my works in one click
faster than the cocaine can cling in gobs
to the sides of my numbed, caking nostrils
like ghouls stuck to the side of that Sinkhole,

too melty to slide down like healthy shits
to the atrium of Hell's rapid heart
pulsating like mirror-tinted windows
that make your clear reflection seem nervous.

I would make my words into relations
that link Us beyond what is referred to
if you'd only be my Friend, like Jesus,
who cripples me with pity, disappears.

10. For the impatient

The shortest distance between two points
is a straight line.

The shortest distance between two points
is -0.000000000000000.

The shortest distance between two points
is zero divided by two.

Or else space folds like pizza
to be eaten more than twice as fast
for less than half the heartburn.

No, the end precedes the beginning—
and that is neither shorter than breath
nor longer than endurance
because it is time made irrelevant.

Mass Merger

11. Bathroom tears

> The way you looked at my tears
> with the detached curiosity of a scientist,
> I knew that I was your shattered mirror
> in which you did not recognize yourself.
>
> Your feelings
> were trying to account for the lack of feeling
> you felt—
> confused feelings that couldn't account for
> the more concrete ones
> you should have, would have or could have felt
> had you been 'yourself'.
>
> Your bathroom tears
> against my crocodile tears
> that show intent rather than pathos,
> *apparently*.

12. Clear the hoard, stat

> She accumulated men in her data hoard
> as passively as she accumulated objects in her apartment,
> the crystallization of her incapacity to say no.
>
> The hoarder
> was buried beneath her inability to distinguish
> trash or treasure.
>
> She could accumulate trash and treasure
> and all the indifferent objects
> that float in the interstices of the two,
> like men,
> without any contradictions or consequences.
>
> But health is loose, remember,

and the hoard didn't interfere with her work,
even if it did determine how her relationships functioned.

She was no free spirit,
but not exactly dysfunctional.

And yet the observer can't distinguish
between an inability and a hard refusal

…we slept, mostly—
maternally ingested by the trash
and amnesia-in-pill-form.

13. "formulaic and lame" irony

Do you want the formula
or the milk—
the two are the same—
or that no two breasts are alike?

Either way, 'natural' or 'free to produce',
you're a baby,
and babies have lame necks and soft heads—
even if their eyes are large.

14. faith walk

At first, you walked all over me.

Without meaning to,
I stuck to the bottom of your shoe
like a child's littered, indigestible sacrament
(gum).

Trash like me comes from a concrete plenitude.

Now, I am with you wherever you go on your faith walk.

And you hate feet…

15. Hit or miss

Sometimes I would fuck her and cum fast,
before she had time to.
Sometimes I'd make her cum,
and I would throb without afterwards.
Sometimes we would both cum,
me usually right after she did.
Sometimes she wouldn't make any noise.
Sometimes I would go soft during,
inside
or when I'd try to change positions.

We talked a lot about murder.
We called ourselves twins and our sex "twincest."

Shit came out when we'd have anal,
but it was my fault
because I could feel her dehydrated, prickly shit
up there with my finger
and I'd stick it up there anyway.

I'd smell it oozing out as she'd cum.
I was the knife loosening her sweeter-than-tomato ketchup,
the anus being a small hole
that gets wider and less sensitive
the further in you go.

This was the precise form
of our relationship as a whole.

The laptop used to breathe and tremble

as its software altered states
when you tickled the keyboard with commands.
It used to vibrate like a living organ.

It isn't the same with the more advanced technology,
whose insides cannot be heard or felt—
like "good" children seen but not heard.

16. The secret of my charm

Like the simulator
whose crazed exactitude must signify that he *really is crazy,*
if I say that I'm charming and I'm lying,
it must be that I *really am charming.*

Charming in my stylized weakness.

Charming when I'm murdery.

Charming when I say
"some people should have been killed at birth"
and mean it.

Charming when I am a better friend
because of the cruelty I discharge privately
on the unnoticeables and unmentionables.

Charming when I throw away recyclables.

Charming when I re-gift
rather than burn the gifts you gave me.

Charming as a somewhat nihilist with self-regard.

Charming when I vote Republican.

Charming when I repeat the things You often said,

Mass Merger

when I am hardened in my creative use
of your soft influences.

Charming when I use your charms on others.

Charming when I became what you wanted,
when you wished without caution.

Charming in my hesitation or my haste.

Charming when I unashamedly
made you sick with yourself.

Charming like Pee-Wee,
the theater masturbator,
climaxing as he got caught.

Charming in my calculated failure
or unwanted success.

Charming inconclusively
in all my provisional assumptions.

Charming when I'm wrong about myself.

...charming than a life ruined by pity,
as childhood ruined by morality that makes boring.

Charming in the wastage of the powers
someone invented to trick the more powerful into equality.

Charming in the breakage
of the hyperbolic silence of the restaurant playlist
with my shrugging, chain wit.

Charming in the unexpected "I know" when you flatter me
that makes you useless.

Charming in my pretentiousness,

Buy Me, Get Me Free

in the matter-of-factness and directness that is obscure.

Charming as a limited edition.

Charming without volume.

Charming n to the n +1th power.

What is the secret of my charm?

You won't find the answer here, only—again—the secret.

Isn't it enough *that* I'm charming?

Isn't it enough *that* there's something
I'm not telling you?

Those Mythbuster nerds are so charmless
that they even make truth undesirable—
truth being a woman.

Some pervert then finds in the ugly truth
his ugly reflection,
makes it even more distasteful for charmers.

Let my poisonous charm
keep me out of the mouth of idiots and equals.
If I'm sweet, let the obese eat me *to death*.
If I'm true, it's because truth is shit without me.
If I'm charming, let it be to baseheads (scholars)
and singular consciences.
Let some take me for better than I am,
let others mistake me for less,
debase me and ruin me for many
(but not for the exceptional).
Let the former rule, or maybe not.

Let the work, *my work*,
work itself out...and work—*for me*.

Mass Merger

If destiny resists my charms,
it's because she's paying attention,
and if she's paying attention,
she must already be charmed.

17. Lays

If they took the chip off my shoulder
and implanted it in my head,
I'd love Lays potato chips and you.

18. Original seduction

God bukkake'd all over Lilith's face,
and the little that oozed into her mouth
and disappeared from view as she swallowed
became the world.

To this day,
no one knows where it ended up,
not even God Himself.

19. Graft titties

Don't wonder if they're fake or real.
It doesn't matter.

They grow ears on the backs of mice.
They already grow entire bodies
with working personalities,
or personalities that are distractions,
from big tits.

The material theses of adequacy of perceptions to reality
and thoughts to perceptions,
must come from those who already suffer
from 'inadequacy'.

20. The polyvalence of breakfast breads

We always have to wait to get in,
and they always rush us to leave.

To *out-flank* you,
I had to become a piece of meat.

21. Swarf

She hated that my spirit
took her breath away/got her choked up,

so she asked me to choke her
and fuck her throat instead.

More anxious than anxious,
she nullified my spirit along with the power she feared…

now I'm anxious;

I had to go choke myself
and fuck myself
to breathe again.

22. a positive out-look

In Heaven,

everything will be interactive
and fully customizable
and fitted, fixed, built-in
and smooth, tight, lubricated.

Maybe that's how it is
when life replaces death
or when death dies.

The eye,
by looking at itself from outside,
out-looks itself—
and sight disappears.

23. Only the pretentious are ashamed of pretentiousness

There is a poetry that sublimates.

There is a poetry that criticizes.

There is a poetry that calls to action.

There is a poetry that unifies.

There is a poetry that redirects.

There is a poetry that arouses.

There is a poetry that 'makes you think'.

There is a poetry that takes the use-value from language,
replaces it with stupid bullshit
and then asks
"You find language, *or me*, trustworthy???"

Most people are unaware of the last type
because they read for pleasure

(including the pleasure
of having one's displeasure confirmed
by reproducing it).

24. Solitarity

From Jesus Christ to JC Penny
on which Lincoln is a mulatto,
where Change is monetary,
they will create a 24-hour news network
that reports on what could have,
would have or should have happened—
a science of Imaginary news.

From Knowledge to "You Know You Want It,"
when coercion lacks Meaning
because the State and the Individual
are Co-conspirators and Co-creators,
because Happiness is undesirable without evidence.

Narcissist, you are but bottled water
on a water planet.

25. Peaceful coexistence

There is no existence
because that is singular and involves enjoyment,
antagonism,
tension.

There is only coexistence,
where pleasing others
is the true function of 'being oneself'.

There can be no peace

Mass Merger

because to want peace
means to be complicit with the system.

If you believe in peace, your penis is a potsticker.

If you believe in peace, your penis is a jalapeño popper.

If you believe in peace, your penis is a peppermint candy
that freshens some someone's breath.

If you believe in peace,
your penis is a pamphlet for timeshares.

If you believe in peace, your penis is your parents.

If you believe in peace,
your penis is the patter of little feet
making privacy more livable.

If you believe in peace,
pucker up for the pathetic pitted against your pleasure,
oriented towards them whether you like it or not.

Integration became a *demand* with manly women;
they discovered history after it no longer meant anything—
after it could no longer speak,
i.e., once it was dead.
Feminism looks like
the formal reinfection of a system
by a dead referential.

If it's not women,
it's Science and Sci-Fi
that 'make us better people
because they make us a better Society',
those two refractory concentrations
of the divine self-reference of liberalism,
by making us neighborly—
that means integrating the phallic into the ludic.

26. Marx in heels

The prostitute checked her phone
in the middle of a job,
and her text message asked a question we all face:
"When do you get off?"

I guess we are, most of us,
masochists on the inside.

27. The Crucial Crushed: The Self-Overcoming of the Clown

Demanding A1 at a top steakhouse.
Demanding cheese as a vegan, vegan 'cheese'.
Liking one trait in someone,
marrying them
and demanding that they drop every other quality.
Picking the songs you like out of the album
to put on your MP3 Player/phone
like picking your favorite passage out of a text
and ignoring the rest—calling *your* reading true.
But you can't pick a line out of a poem,
a moment out of a trajectory,
an identity out of a process,
one sense over all the others
(other than 'good sense', but that isn't educable).

The same people have axiomatized sex, joy
and the sublime—
whatever that means.
In that movement, they also sexualized the axiom
(or poetic fragment)
to my advantage.

They are murderers of the real
because that is what is *realistic* for them,
or *in reach*.

The only thing they Hate more than 'Genius'
is Accidentality.

28. nihilism, perfect for cocktail parties

   Nihilists still have nothing to look forward to.

   I am not that optimistic.

29. sometimes I root for terrorists

   Blame the American entertainment morality
   for habituating me to always rooting for the underdog.

   But because revolutions can't happen in a vacuum,
   we have random acts of terror,
   which accomplish as much partying.

30. E Money

   He loves heroin, cocaine and strippers,
   but has a good job,
   a college degree
   and has never been to jail.

   Everyone resents him
   because he doesn't answer or return their phone calls.

   Concern can be a clever mask for murder.

   He just wants to live
   at the agnostic scale
   at which boobs are hard to tell from butts.

Our solutions are usually displacements
of the question.

31. Disturbing the peace

The people on the lake
complain a lot about noise
and file lawsuits...but mostly complain.
Several people agree.
They asked politely, but they are entitled residentially.
Someone is going to get shot, and they are wrong.
They don't have the right.
People have rights to peace,
and mostly they are entitled.

They talk a lot,
complain a lot
and disturb *my* peace.

I laugh and entertain them with louder questions.
I don't sue or complain.

32. Group speak

I have always been content to keep silent
wherever there has been an overabundance of words—
to let talkers talk, without exactly listening,
but better, letting them believe I'm listening,
that 'them' they place within me
like a card swallowed by an ATM,
disappearing only to be spit back out.

Tending is the Accidental,
the ineffable,

a predilection to imperviousness.
Pre-tending is training for work (leisure),
a subordinate activity given categorically
to children by adults
whose language has grown too exact
to understand irony or play.

33. Simulcast

Can you live at the level of the general
without being generic?

Can you fold on a royal flush?

How long before you flush the perfect shit?

Does your feeling have the exaggerated intensity
of a massage oil for *her* pleasure?

Are you a politician flip-flopping and testing
how the truth-effect affects the audiences?

Does your language only refer to itself?

Will you duplicate or replicate?

Is this a new-look for you?

Are there enough layers, textures or tones?

Are you cut?
(By which I do not mean in spectacular shape.)

Are you giving me a discount?

What is the rate at which you love?

Is this a game or a show or both,
on which I am the first contestant?

If I contest you, will I make it to the next episode?

Do you need verification?

Does it matter if this is *real*?

Does this *work*?

Is this arranged?

34. Two dicks

What happens when you take a metaphor for a reality,
for a meaning?

You clone your phallus
and get it surgically added to your body
above the first one,
so you can double penetrate your wife
without the need for a dildo
or another person.

35. Stuff and things

Her hairs were stuck to the shower
like the spaghetti thrown at the walls to see if it's ready.
I was always packing up my things then unpacking them.
She always asked me to leave
and called to ask me to come back
just when I'd get on the highway.
When she wouldn't let me leave,
I'd break "stuff and things"—

what she always said every time I asked
what she was thinking about.

36. Stool sample

Even shit can become a discourse.
They will even analyze it in a lab
and extend linguistics to it.
They will analyze its structure and its message.
They will make it signify.
Some will argue for its internal coherence.

Even shit can become functional.
The Japanese have learned how to make burgers with it.
It is full of probiotics.
Shit is good for stimulating growth, like everything.
Coprophagia is the summit of recycling.

Someone has definitely written a book
called *What Your Shit Says About You*...

you will be able to personalize it with a special diet,
and it will become worth talking about—
in a matter-of-fact manner,
lacking all humor or perversion.

Monkeys will still use it to mock us.

37. Other than death

The virtual is the medium
whose messages can be consumed without dying.

The female is the organism
whose organ can weaken her cyclically

without killing her.

We fear both more than death.

But really,
that is just what language says now,
historically.

38. Muse…um

The people walk through the streets,
through *the people*,
squinting and nodding.
The art gallery opens gynecologically into the streets.

"When everyone is constantly taking pictures of you,
it's natural to want to change things about yourself,"
said a Kardashian before the laser altered her curvature
by miniaturizing her cells.

White people use facial cream
that can cause death by diarrhea
(which the Blacks die of in third world countries),
then donate vitamins
to those countries where the Blacks are starving to death.

The phallus is a loaded question.

39. Learn how to learn

You have to be taught how to learn,
and the bare-ass belt treatment is the first lesson…
it will teach you how to respond to questioning—
yes sir or no ma'am;
they always force you out of your silence

to tell them what they want to hear
(the answer to their question);
you must pay them
(a value they have determined in advance)
with their own currency
or you won't get across the bridge.

Trolling them works, but at your *expense*...
since even *'beating them at their own game'*
means being economical, i.e., moral,
since the moral is the treat given
to an interpretive job well-performed,
like the pleasure is the treat given
to a sexual job well-performed.

But life is still the remainder of an incomplete suicide,
and the fool is still the one
who knows too much to speak
and yet can't keep his mouth shut.

40. Just do it. Nothing matters, not even nothing.

Shia Labeouf said "cybernetics"
and "gaming" and "feedback loops,"
so I will no longer say those.

There should be a blog that can be read live as it's written.
The simultaneity of reading and writing,
already simultaneous in the head of the writer,
will show the absurdity of being on either side.

When reader and writer are joined,
so that nothing remains of either, there is poetry.

Poetry is still not a green screen, though,
because it doesn't liberate art as value...
because art is dumb,

but not *mere dumbness.*

41. irruption, eruption, interruption

>We want to have one another
>and consume one another too—
>we take bites out of each other's organs
>to reach the nugget inside
>and reduce each other's surface area to half,
>and like a river thinned by the channel,
>we flow faster.
>We flow faster in descent, too.
>
>Nothing new enters without space
>and no space exists that isn't cleared,
>so nothing new enters without something destroyed.
>Something forgotten,
>something experienced and swallowed—
>that itself must leave
>to clear the way for new ingestions.
>
>Indigestion kills the appetite—
>the appetite kills indigestion.
>Who knows?
>
>Poetry never sounded more stupid,
>more like an illness.
>But despair taken beyond guilt
>expropriates the attraction to guilt—
>that dumb complicity with neuronal enslavement
>to a false bottom that demands that the summit,
>'guiltlessness',
>too is a limit...
>a cloud that, like distance, negates visibility
>and thereby increases curiosity.
>
>We consume each other and grow

and shit out ourselves and each other.
We are always out of each other's reach
and re-strategize in flux that isn't radical.
But meaning is given in complete, coherent sentences—
so there is continuity of conversation.

She treats me like something when I am nothing.
There is no clearly defined me, in me—
but there is that in her.
But there isn't because we continue speaking
and she understands me—she moves with me.

I can never satisfy her
because I cannot be satisfied with me—
the I that precedes the me in the discourse,
always separated by the action and the description.
She can never satisfy me.

We leave each other hungry
and that is key (to what?).

42. For the interviewer

What had happened was
I aimed at the accident and failed—
not willingly, on purpose or even knowingly
(thinking *without precedent* that I succeeded,
or thinking *in succession*).

Offering only excuses,
I am not answerable for *what* had happened.

'Creation' is only conveyed in myth—
a conveyor belt of myth and maintenance,
where keeping the story straight
incriminates more quickly.

Thought itself is an event,
the unfolding in itself of effects.
"I think; therefore, I do not exist."
That's no better than the other.

Neither caused nor causal,
Thought is worldly—
and the world not being a screen,
Thought cannot be out-thunk.

Challenging it to exist,
one traces its disappearance.

What fish can swim against the current
without jumping out of water?

43. I thought you wanted to be alone with me

Somehow "putting yourself out there"
came to mean proliferating everywhere.
You meet no one on the path to nowhere
when you're not a legit victim de guerre.

Groped by crowds over which you surf,
"making others money for lack of self-worth" is cliché,
meet me deadly beyond the spotlight by day
where vision doesn't fire that isn't cockeyed first.

44. Indifference and complicity

To follow the fly darting across the room with her eyes,
her eyes dart rapidly back and forth,
and her head twitches instead of rotating,
just like a fly's.

This is only problematic if values are considered.

With values, it's difficult to be oblivious.
Either way, even flies can play with you…
which is to say, disrupt your concentration.

45. Love that works

She loves me
and is committed to me
insofar as she is a masochist
whose hope is for me to break her heart.

Being a sadist,
I bar her from that enjoyment,
keep loving her and defer her pleasure forever.

That is why our relationship *works*.

46. Translation of a death poem

Death. Death. Death. Death.
Death. Death. Death. Death.
Death. Death. Death. Death.
Death. Death. Death. Death.
Death. Death. Death. Death.
Death. Death. Death. Death.
Death. Death. Death. Death.
Death. Death. Death. Death.

…

Do you still want to call it a detour?
What's the point of reading it then,
you deciphering asshole?

You will never translate it:
"Fuck you, reader."
Because even the fuck you is a form of justification...
for *you*.

48. Two lines to snort

Sex produces the orgasm, jouissance.
But eroticism seduces enjoyment and lasts.

"Impatient cokeheads don't snort the shorter line"
doesn't apply here.

49. Trying not to dream

Poems are faster than the analytic process
and terrorize like a leaked photo album
until they disrupt the mental apparatus,
poisoning more quickly than dental amalgams.

The sudden flood of the repetition
interrupts that singular ethical question.
Medusa, catching herself in the mirror,
hardens from how much *she* fears *her*.

In the dream, I could be your anyone;
I could even inevitably *be you*.
And upon waking you escape the only one
responsible for working through.

Poems reveal too much too quickly
and actually end up setting you back.
So, you continue living sickly
and actively on the attack.

Mass Merger

I feel what I imagine is having been raped,
having become your transferal—projection.
It's like my speech was previously taped
or live with a delay—if need be, corrected.

I *became* the monster you saw me as.
You were creative at being neurotic.
"Breaking hearts in a lasting fashion" has
become for you a 'skill', not just a habit.

Your father lives in excruciating pain
too proud to take medication.
Now, are you *accidentally* the same?
Is that not your myopic edification?

Who is good? Elvis, the Frenchman, pop, *not* you.
That's only according to *your own* view.
Thinking you're shit, you really become it—
and your actions make your self-image legit.

So, my kindness comes as a foreign body,
an intentional attack on your autonomy—
and, by making *me* into *what* you fancy,
you keep me out of your empty pantry.

'Don't love me! Don't love me! Don't!'
You imply that I'm a threat to your wont.
Once I'm finally at a comfortable distance,
you describe your dreams, force me to listen.

In all our accumulating mail, there's proof—
that of your former love I'm a spoof.
You'll know exactly why "*It* went wrong."
You *grill* your past…and so handle it with tongs.

'Finish the dream!' I seemed to be crying out,
the completion of which is me, stabbed to death.
In it, I encourage you to endure your vision quest:

Buy Me, Get Me Free

that maybe your anger is what you're anxious about.

I will not judge you for your anger towards me—
I am another older man that grabbed you sleepily,
that pinned you down with my body of work, too.
Instead of blaming him, it's me you'll sue.

I will gladly embody the ghost of your enemy
and let you send *me* away instead—
because we're just *two individuals* inevitably,
which contradicts the I love you's you said.

I thought I was the saddest person I've met
until I experienced your fatherly disease
that increases guilt the more you do as you please
and fills you with a victim's *regret*.

Who punishes, who receives it, who are you?
And *which side are you on* in the inner zoo?
How do you know yours is the right rendition
when you seem *always* in the fight position?

Anxiety always leaves you prepared.
Ironically, you feel safe when you're always scared.
And when you forget that there is a *"differently,"*
you recriminate, longing for the penitentiary.

You stab me repeatedly, with efforts otherwise,
and in the interstice between dream and wake,
you try to avoid both the real *and* the fake.
So which is it, is your violence automatic or wise?

The parts of the dream were conflicting—
and sure, *that* makes it interesting!
But are you not actively trying to *not dream*
as I encourage "Risk it! Hurt me!" comfortably.

Wanting to kill me, sleep with me *and* wake up
from a dream in which you *frighten yourself*—

Mass Merger

your capacity for evil and your capacity for love,
two strengths that must grow *together* to grow well.

Half-way between one and the other,
you destroy *both* in their felicity.
And clearly you must have resented me
for being killed doesn't make *me* shudder...

Whether I laugh *with you* or *at you*—
that is the ambiguity of the dream.
Could I think you're silly or cute to eschew
the fact that you may *want* to murder me?

You are alone, "want to be alone *with* me;"
in the dream, you get both equivalently.
Maybe you just refuse to believe
that anyone could love someone *ferociously*.

Maybe you think I stand on sleeping legs
or that I'm Zarathustra standing on the ledge
and you're my eagle and my snake,
this rambling fool with theories half-baked.

Do not the intelligent deserve *their* folly?
Likewise, don't the fools deserve their wisdom?
I'm a slave before Cleopatra, kneeling.
Your pleasure is my pins and needles feeling.

When the bad has presumably stolen your freedom,
send the good away to *prove* you "don't need them."
After all, maybe you feel powerful again
from killing who may be your one true friend.

Maybe I'm playing Caesar to your Brutus,
who you must kill to say, "Recognize me."
Perhaps I laugh *at* you for an immoderate fuss—
you *do* think I don't take your pain seriously...

50. NOLA, not only laughter annuls

There are people quieter than I
who are ok with dying
because they enjoy their respectable lives.

Me?
The cockroaches eat my skin
that peeled off because I got drunk and fell asleep
on someone else's boat
off beer that I didn't pay for or thank anyone for.

I live with my lover who dislikes the taste of water.

David,
the man who plays a battery-powered Casio keyboard
on his porch at night
in an uptown house the Whites do Elvis karate for
in their minds,
saved my life with his government-bought smartphone
in exchange for 6 American Spirit,
hippie-killer,
menthols.

Am I *really* grateful for these Things?
To whom or for what?

I can never tell, or never prove it,
so I generally don't worry about it,
value.

Graciousness is a useless demand
for a response that's already automatic.

51. The beauty of appearances

The men are always about to cum,

Mass Merger

The women are always cumming.
The 'man' has a future, lacks cunning.
The 'woman', in the present, isn't one.

The 'true' beauty of appearances
is that you need not believe in beauty,
but can let others believe in it
and perform the *label* 'cutie'.

She can only cum out of her mind,
only leaves her mind when cumming.
She has no nature, it's assigned—
not alienated, just becoming.

52. We sport Events like fashion

The lights are tiresome blush on my face.
The stage—the court—
becomes a screen, the Ground, during the pre-game,
the pre-eminence of the game.
You can feel the sound-system inside you.

The junior cheerleaders shake their booties,
neither pushed not active,
dancing in celibate promiscuity
like money.
They are going to put a woman's face on the 20$ bill
because a little girl wrote the white house,
though sexuality is not monistic
and misunderstood childishly—
because childhood exists as what copies copiers.

The teams, less than different,
fraternize and 'defeat' without principle.

We have swapped the transcendental
for the visceral—

without chills.

How much better, I think, would bloodsport be?
Death is too invisible...
unlike repulsion, which is obvious.

We fear seduction, the vague quasi-answer
the corresponding actions to which are damning.

53. Time contracts like a disease, swells like a diseased organ

    I have lived the free time of a 100-year-old man
    and have already accomplished my life's work
    at 27.
    I still exist, but I'm not sure I'm still alive,
    having accomplished my life's work already.
    I have the free time of a geriatric in a home
    and approach work with the same useless,
    nostalgic performativity.

    Time has shortened
    from the book
    to the play
    to the movie
    to the television show
    to the clip
    to the Vine video
    in negative correspondence
    to the lengthening of the free time,
    like the shortening of the diameter of the arteries
    corresponds positively
    to the lengthening of the waist size.

    Now, I live like a man on the moon
    or a brain in a vat.
    If I had Alzheimer's,
    at least things would appear new to me,

like myself.

54. Healthy gambling habits

> The best way to wager your health
> is to have unprotected sex.
> The pleasant anxiety of the clinic
> turns corpses into plush dolls
> like hermaphrodites in India.

55. .com Mode

> Only one person can sit on the commode at a time,
> the prototypical commodity.
>
> My toilet signifies that my shit smells better than yours.
>
> See, the basic unit of 'Humanity' is two.

56. Fuck Hemingway or women, whichever

> I want to be a housewife
> and watch TV while I do menial tasks
> that waste my talents and libido
> until my brain loses carbonation
> and its syrup becomes denser and separates from the water.
>
> I want to be a housewife
> whose labor cannot be converted into use-value
> and whose exchange-value gets away from her
> the less she does or says.
>
> I want to be a housewife

Buy Me, Get Me Free

who doesn't read books
but handles the money.

I want to be a housewife.
Unliberated.
Undesiring.
Mute—except for flirtatious wit I share with my husband,
who never acknowledges it.
And wit has no repressed or history or end.

I want to be a housewife
with a closet that has a closet
in a house that has rooms that serve no purpose,
rooms that you can see but can't get to.

I want to be a housewife who throws food away,
leaving nothing to chance.

I want to be a housewife
and mock the laws you try to attach to me
by proving them 'right'.

I want to be a housewife with a college degree I can't use,
one which I 'worked toward'
with no intention of getting anything out of it.

I want to be a housewife who's perfectly content
and therefore impossible to escape.

I want to be a housewife—
that is, anything but a cause.
Perfectly uninvolved, cynical,
nodding, smiling and discriminatory—
without conviction or argument.

I want to be a housewife—withdrawn and extrapolated.
Perfectly deserted. Impassable.

I want to be a housewife to the nth power,

raised like a fakir's rope.

Masturbating once in a day—that's pathetic.
But masturbating ten times—that's masterful.

57. Realized eschatology

>A "good time," that equivalent unit,
>reproduces the moral Code of fun
>and accumulates like genes at the Crime—
>those generous gods of "in other news."
>
>Involve ourselves indiscriminately
>with the indifference of happenings
>that pool like *money*, without a plural
>or a destructive hermeneutic.
>
>The tautology of Reality
>that has no counter-discourse, counter-gift,
>finds its autistic perfection in the
>non-event that repeats like episodes.
>
>The primary narcissism of TV
>completes one with oneself, the same thing
>as conversion—the picture in picture
>of self-image assumes self-consciousness.
>
>With you, the hegemony is broken
>by something that cannot happen again
>because it begins in death. Memory's
>hand is forced by what's Other than info.
>
>Why remember what's reproducible,
>can be revisited like a homepage,
>that new, lite womb that's faster than recall?
>You are immortal *because* you can leave.

Buy Me, Get Me Free

Being with you forever, that sacred
ring that binds us, two singularities,
is destined only because we do end—
unlike the party—in presence, in death.

The event cannot be controlled. Science
would prove us right insofar as we react
in a vacuum, which is a flawless victory
because time is sucked out with the stakes.

Our love is imperfect, unlike cosmetics,
because it has no counterpart in speech—
it's pathos amounts to the valueless
element that makes it undeniable.

The feelings are caught, coming from above,
by bullied children whose gloves cover their
faces out of fear, the miraculous
element of Chance's thoughtless arrow

leans into a miscalculated chink,
whose wound goes far without feeling, until
it cannot be stitched—when the new wounded
dies fatally without signs of decline.

58. The Iconoclastic Drive

If I rolled in our love like a happy dog,
it's that it was dead
because you disappeared behind your selfies—
meaning in the Desert.

With form-for-form's-sake,
the arbitrary word revenges *out of the blue*
for its being *used*—
as if it *could be* used, another mistake.

Mass Merger

It grants you a wish—its candles in one blow—
that comes true only for immediate forms
of *Thought Not Radical*, out of stir with worlds.

You let me see you die,
the one *unlawful* Thing—not *unruly*.

59. By the time

What do I do with myself?
More time than a loitering beggar.
At least I don't have any crude wealth
and need not sieve through a ledger.

Community often occurs through work.
I avoid both, do neither. I'm a jerk!
A drain on the economy, the libidinal,
and my depression isn't even seasonal.

Honestly, I'm a malingering bum.
Without even any pressure, I'm the mung.
I demand the charity of your knickers—
were it to grow more intimate, we'd bicker.

Mowing lawns, picking weeds, washing cars,
I don't stimulate the economy, don't "go hard."
Hipsters demonstrating in sweatshop ensembles,
look hip even when, at loss of cause, they mumble.

I'd easily have joined the 'twenty-seven club'
if where my head should be there wasn't a nub.
Once I've gnawed at all my cuticles,
I'm too accepted by the beautiful.

What does it mean "to be accomplished?"
I think it probably means "to be dead."
Spent, exhausted and attractively famished,

they're stupid, sure—but I'm stuck in my head.

Spindling, unused, worthless legs—
but with scars that say, "I live on the edge."
(Perhaps only the edge of the commode.)
Primping, I run late; fashionably, I never go.

I don't believe that I'm significant.
I certainly can't trust *you*, loyal sycophant.
I'm the mitt you use to open the iron oven—
the past—to remember hotter, unburnt lovers.

60. Faster than speed

Someone wrote some books on speed.

Someone was even a prophet of speed.

So, I can write some poems on speed,
and they will be in style.

What if things are so fast
that even speed has gone out of style?

I came late too quickly.

61. gain, again, against

The purpose of Life cannot be to *gain* something—

since Life is ultimately lost and all.

But then *again*, Death is no argument *against* it.

62. the Doofus

Because of how *we* think,
he is due for a fuss—
and if he doesn't, he must
be ignorant or afraid.

Luckily, he has Us—
appointed by the Law—
to speak in his behalf.
He'll catch up on our terms.

If he could speak before God and did
without asking for anything,
he would offend our haste—
bench-warming thoughtlessly (unthinkably).

And there will always be
future doofuses
that will waste on that bench,
credited with their Team's win

because of *our* need.

63. I don't care that I suck because I don't care

The bootstrappers say the sun rises with or without you,
and if you can't beat time, you should join it.
Whether sun morality or fun morality,
you're supposed to get yourself out of bed.
Doers apparently drink the vinegar…
but does it taste sweet?
They are too happy to be happy. I don't trust that.
I have found *them*
with looks on their faces sourer than mine,
and I could pretty much despair over nothing in particular
(so anything or whatever).

I've learned the day goes on without me just fine.
I've also learned a woman's floating terror or despair
that seems to unload itself at the most mundane things
can take you to heights,
so long as you hold off.

64. It could be worse, considering

    I wanted to be loved in a discriminatory way,
    not in terms of a verbal agreement
    or craft.
    Nevertheless, love is an abstract term
    that can be 'applied' indiscriminately
    to a person, thing or idea
    without any contradiction.
    Terms cruelly terminate.
    Love freely exterminates.
    An energy invested.
    An energy withdrawn.
    An energy of the conjunction
    [Holocaust & corn-cob].

    I have considered that all items at McDonald's
    taste like McDonald's, breakfast and lunch—
    all the sign 'McDonald's'.
    The ham tastes like the burger patty,
    the egg like the ketchup—
    maybe the cheese is the common denominator,
    but that's just what they want you to (rationally) think.
    All the little signs, the individual items,
    Megatron up
    to the genome of Mickey D's.
    I'm always eating the medium,
    the level at which all messages are the same,
    thinking I'm eating the message in its ironic variety—
    but all my crap is the same.

Be careful getting too close to the sacred—
it becomes profane.
Like how when you get too close to the profane,
it becomes sacred.
Zoomed in up close, everything looks the same—
money or microscope.

Nobody wants that shit.

65. Hands off time off

When *the clock* has too much time on its hands,

it's time to stop working.

66. Medium fits all

One day the dead brought the living to trial before God,
who mediates reality, or the disjunction between terms.

God's messages (his subjects)
once still contradicted one another.
Living and dead waged playful wars against one another,
and were rivals become friends (even greater rivals).

Because God reproduced himself in all his messages,
the living no longer felt special,
so they banished the dead,
stopped playing with them
and began competing against them for totality.

The dead, no closer to God than the living,
felt excluded by God
because of their exclusion from the living.

So, they asked God to neutralize the privilege of the living
so that the dead were equal to the living.

The living went on living death
as a consequence of the dead's dying to live,
and the dead were as content as the living,
who eventually stopped feeling their indifference.

Although the dead were no longer alienated
and were equal to the living,
they quickly learned
they no longer carried the same force they once did…
and just as the living had no force of their own,
the dead could no longer have sovereignty.

They were treated with the ludic fascination
of by-gone objects.
They could even be resurrected,
never either living nor dead,
since they were retro from the get-go.

God died before he could reverse the sentence,
and from then on
synthesis and indifference could no longer be disentangled.

67. Thoughts after jogging

Things must be taken apart
before they can be synthesized,
must be coded before they can be decoded.

There is neither part nor whole in the code,
because a unity only exists between separate parts—
but the code is the same in 'all the parts'.

I have learned from jogging
there is no endurance

other than simulated, extended performance.
Endurance is oriented continuously towards some end,
but performance only *performs itself*
reproductively.

I've heard of the "runner's high."
It's a sado-masochistic synthesis of pleasure and pain—
which, after the two terms are ruptured
and pitted against one another,
amounts to the non-contradiction of the two.
When pleasure and pain played off one another,
and so reciprocated one another,
they were partnered.
When pleasure and pain competed separately for reality,
they were fused—indistinct.

I haven't felt the runner's high of "I did that."
I haven't felt the abreactive high
of the perfect functioning of the body,
the leisurely high of an excess energy
wasted on *action pour l'action*
or that of the near-death high
of an erotic cardio-vascular system,
or the cozy, snug high of lifeless exhaustion.

I have felt the indifference of a body that runs,
and that is *all*.

68. Diarhetoric

Lacking moral fiber,
the poetic is a laxative
that turns gold (mac n'cheese) to liquid cash
and liquid cash to virtual money.
The poetic is never 'at work'.
The poetic is not designed,
but stirred like chicken eggs—

saying nothing about the randomness or cause of fortune.
The poetic is not edited
or shifted
or pulsed—
but re-wagered, interrupted frivolously.

Still, poets will lie
and call their 'creative' wastage "hard work"
and their shit "meticulous…"

as if one has control over the form of their excrement.

They *must* lie if they are to become Heroes…
the people love authority;
they demand speech writers
and won't pay for bottled farts.

They'll pay for bottled water though.

And they'll see nature as a system…
of production…
that wastes nothing, uses everything (including space).

They functionalize everything.

69. Agape b roll

She never got me to eat her out
right after someone else had cum inside her
without knowing,
but she easily could have.

Only the wounded, agape, can appreciate love…

because even their wounds
are challenges to love and seduce more.

70. Sweet evil

>Like ass-eating, I'm assumed dirty,
>but I'm sweet as anti-freeze—
>a taste you cannot forget.
>
>Because only flavors come in varieties.

71. Homeomorphin' power rangers

>You think working is hard,
>try doing nothing.
>
>You think doing nothing is hard,
>try not thinking.
>
>You think not thinking is hard,
>try thinking about nothing.
>
>You think that's hard,
>try doing nothing about it.
>
>(*In case you were thinking about it,
>not trying doesn't work, either.*)

72. death is probably healthier than life

>I didn't come here
>to participate in the Group Therapy session
>called Life Behind the Scenes.
>
>They can't exactly kick me out of it.
>They are too committed.
>
>They can only move me

from institution to institution
for as long as my welcome lasts.

They mop up the downer trail
I leave with liquid used to blow bubbles
that cannot be used to clean with.

73. What difference does *it* make?

Absent-minded, the heart grows fonder of thought.

I'll do anything for you,
but that's the only way I'll do anything—
because I refuse to do things I chose for myself.

I am seduced by you, but it's nothing *you've done.*

My seduction lacks a Reason and a History.

74. Unreachable earth-like planets

She shattered my heart with inconsistency and shock,
what anxiety could never prepare me for.

I shattered her phone, to erase all traces of myself,
to withdraw my closest proximity
and afford my most nebulous distance,
so she couldn't hoard me, have me
and eat me too.

I ripped up all the letters,
which bear the specific mark of their author,
so the fragments of each letter
could not be distinguished one from the other.
They were more important to her than all the hoard—

data or object hoards.

Instead of disappearing from her life,
through the destruction of my artifacts,
she couldn't get me out of her mind.

She couldn't mourn me
without the artifices of a hermeneutics.
She was in the limbo of seduction,
where uncertainty dissolves anality
into the pleasure of submission.

Death worked with me for once,
taking the credit for Disappearance—
which no one and nothing can be responsible for,
since only objects can 'do' it, making Death even obsolete.

75. You are the dream whose attraction disappears with interpretation

The world is a whore who, totally yours,
which is to say valueless
(or of a subjective value that's worthless),
will put on any outfit for you
as you stare squinted,
shocked that your commands work,
that she falls for them, for your power,
that concept you simulated and she *realized*.

But she puts on the outfits, carelessly and complicitly,
only to take them off for you,
when she is always stripping
but never bare.

She is perfect
because she puts her clothes on
right after you fuck her.

76. blue beak of the flame

Exhausting ourselves,
pecking out the superficial vitality of our reflections
whose accusatory depth
angers us in the sunlit window pane,
all our lives we are hysterical bluebirds
whose lives dramatize the blackmail
of the occupants of the house—us.

It's quite humorous what is sad is stupid—

that is, elsewhere than…

77. Burden of proof

We keep hard cash in circulation
to deny the absence of money,
which no one believes in any longer as they swipe.

I could live off credit forever,
never work a single day—
as the days fold into one another
like the sides of a crystal Rubik's cube
whose indeterminacy begets logical sequences—
and no one would be able to tell
because I would be the same person,
and perfectly unrecognizable *as usual*.

I become more and more skeptical
about the reality of reality—
I challenge skepticism with skepticism
and reality with thoughtlessness
and play off the other.

I don't believe in the value of a dollar.

So I might as well waste it on you—
proving that Chance doesn't exist.

78. Ceres' money

In our 'private room', we are both man, both woman,
both animal, both god, both goddess—
sometimes we are the relations between these.

We resemble each,
connoting all and denoting nothing.

When we act freely,
we have no fixed, internalized value
but no *merely temporary, temperamental* values either.

When freedom became a value,
the only thing left to do was shop alone.

We offer; we don't refer.
Here, we are gifts and oblations.

God circulates in Spirit *with* Us
instead of watching,
that is, judging and remaining unaffected.

79. Consult the literature

They all want experts because the reproduction
occurs at the time of production, not after.

They all want to be experts
because the simulation occurs before production,
not with it.

The enjoyment, shit the orgasm itself,
follows a garrulous performance, a moan or a mechanism
or a redundant gyration pattern.

Because it is either a sound,
a language of pleasure
or a pattern of movement,
cumming can become a science, a technique.

The orgasm streamlined by a bibliography
a recitation,
copycat
or by a choreography.

The orgasm was once a break.
Now it is a fulfillment,
an expected outcome of a manual that imposes a model…
an Ikea of labor that breaks things into steps
and empowers you by letting you be the maker.

80. If I'm lying, I'm dying. If I'm not, she is.

She hates when I say things
and do not do them.

Luckily, she doesn't know
that when I do do them,
giving the sayings whatever arbitrary referent she needs,
I'm only giving the sayings an alibi
to continue to be said.

I don't mind giving my words artificial depth
by realizing them.

If it's reality that seduces her, so be it.

She can have it however she wants it,

and that is the secret to my words—

that she dies by them.

81. Death sentence

In language, death always gets the *last word*.

82. This time

This time she isn't an avatar
for which the effortful design gave way critically
to a randomized appearance the gamer commits herself to
for the duration of the game.

This time she isn't one of those dead space islands
that divide the parking spaces,
covered topically with neutral pine needles.

This time I see something in her eyes
other than the objects behind my back.

This time, the shit will have an out-of-body experience.

83. All I gave her was my all

She was a commercial that could make me cry—
the hysteresis and blackmail
of the statistical medium.

All her charity did was teach me that I was poor,
when before I never thought of my poverty.

All she shared with me
was my poverty and her 'richness'—
richer than a glob of triple chocolate cake
that retains the flaccidity of the batter.

84. the bar

Sometimes I try to piss or shit my pants,
just to see if I can
(like how people climb Everest).

It turns out I can't seem to do it.

I am not free…

why would I want to be something I'm not?

85. ass to mouth

And what if you based your diet
on the smelliness of your shit?

Who then would be healthy—vegies or meaties?

But then nothing would be fit for consumption.

And even the nothing-eaters would expel air!

86. Science or religion?

Turning away from *what matters*
to attend to *material*

or turning away from *the material*
to attend to *what matters more?*

87. Hellacious

> If I'm going to hell,
> that's probably because I've never been there,
> or at least that I'm not there now.
>
> I must be in heaven, then.

88. in no sense (innocence)

> My life is murder porn
> at which the moralists' interpretations
> are disappointed in advance
> (as they are made in advance)—
>
> I never murder anyone.
>
> Passion is not fast enough
> to be an antecedent reality,
> and prejudice is no more intended,
> no less lubricious and potent
> than pre-cum.
>
> I take my revenge
> in the truthfulness they nullify me (encode me) with
> by disappointing them *with truth—at truth.*
>
> And all this *unintentionally!*
> That is, without an actor's flare—
> like regular porn
> without an explosive (or cloudy) cumshot,
> porn in which the cum has the *clarity* of the medium!

I commit a greater crime than murder—
I am not entertaining…
not as welcoming as a murderer,
whose story is *inviting*.

I incriminate the viewer
with the greatest of all crimes:

not to be entertained…

89. Meta-servitude

Having reached the limit of service,
we have 'invented' a service-begetting serf
whose job it is to find others jobs.

This coming from a species
whose self-contempt has reached such a height
that individuals martyr themselves for—
and commit their lives to—
saving the lives of animals…
without even a preference *for which* animal species,
for they *All equal Us* in their unfreedom.

So far below Good and Evil have we sunk
that we exalt *Nature*—
and all its bastard 'creations'
we suspect it to have left on our accessible doorstep
like bewildering bags of shit
without the innocence of experimental humor—
above culture,
and most of all, above ourselves
(being nothing but social instruments).

Those who claim to dance above this whole victim order
only dance the way serious and feeble old maids

Mass Merger

    stomp on flaming bags of shit on their doorsteps…

    and who would want to ruin their blue suede shoes!?

    (In the end, Elvis could only interpret himself
    as an instrument of the people.
    He died *from nothing* at the height of his wealth—
    which, according to his fans,
    meant in the service of another
    who didn't reciprocate his love.)

90. My game is weaker than yours. I don't win, but neither do you (and that's better than victory because it's cruel).

    Is there nothing more boring?
    There is nothing more fascinating—
    like endoscopy.
    I'm *dead serious*,
    and I build my life only like movie sets are built,
    quickly and with the assumption
    that people are manipulable.

    I'm on a water diet of tabloid dailiness.

    Will there be politics my whole lifetime?

    It has no reason to end.

    It has no reason to continue.

    It has no reason to do anything,
    and conspiracy would only make it respectable.

    I'm a political agnostic.

    I will only vote for Donald Trump,
    because, like a woman who has turned out well,

Buy Me, Get Me Free

I play, have always played,
with a full deck of cards…

and because he is more realistic, curious, experimental
as a reality TV sensate
than the hardened Machiavellian.

Skeptic? Agnostic?

Political ecstasy is cute
because the Many makes mini-.
I respond well to the childish honesty
that I'm surrounded by nothing but toys
in everyday life,
from the microwave to the policeman.
I live the everyday dangerousness
of giddily discovering I'm in a movie
I don't know the script to
and cannot even transcribe.
I'm cooler than you
because I don't know the rules to my game
but am not an anarchist.
And the excess of information
you don't know how to manage
with your morbid paradigm of meaning
made *me* freer from information—
lighter but not so light that I defy gravity and volition
(whatever volition is).

I'm less driven than you,
and I'll get what you want because of it, stupid.

Truth is on the tip of my tongue
when I burnt it eating pizza faster than a download.

If the moral of the political game
is to win over the masses,
then the farce is its best player
(who as a farce plays the historical game in better taste

Mass Merger

than any *progressive*).

I am participating in a self-destructive system
in the process of *undoing*
or effortless wiki-action.
I follow the instincts.
I do not miss you or anyone,
but I am not exotic…nor erotic.

I am stoically interesting.
Behind the mask, I'm a bore or not even a bore—
as if you could ever get *that* far
to the center of *this* sucker
with only licks
and no bites.

I have pressed my heart into coal
to smoke the meatiness of my carcinogenic, tasty Thought.
My *fatum* has never been BPA-free
(*Buyer's Purchase Agreement*),
and contains fluid-thinking
I would risk death than sterilize with UV lighting.
I am bluer than UV.

I had to kill you to love again,
to be tastefully cruel again.

Your impoverishing love
made me more refined and lovable, you cheat.

I would make a great politician,
skeptic of audacious manliness,
to your Seussical, involuted bow
behind which the curtain drops.

Enemy of your enemy,
your friend who frees you from copycat
by not being original—
a mock-up from birth.

Buy Me, Get Me Free

Slip on my creative juices—
I am a racial slur, a "banana"...
eastern on the outside, western on the inside,
potassium preservative
and sugar-producing decay.

91. thoughts in poem are closer than they appear

She was despicable,
hateful,
reputation-obsessed,
as saintly as any passive sodomite.

If you get too much sun, you get cancer.
Too much Medium: too little death for decadence.
If you are prone to mellow-noma
(low-energy law),
receive too much good
and *cellular you* exits time,
loses death and becomes endless,
a monstrous, waste-less (and appetite-less) outcrop
of yourself—
infinite and with a single message,
with semantic equality,
with an equivalence of being to time.

What else would you expect
from a body whose image is revered
only insofar as it illuminates others—
a medium with no message of its own,
not even the one *it* is?

Woe to that disturbing light
that *demands* reverence
in exchange for the *necessary* lack of reverence
it has for itself,

Mass Merger

which must perish
as surely as the light *it must* throw on others grows.

What cruel and unusual spirit hasn't thought to itself
"Your enjoyment of me
ruins my own enjoyment of myself,
for you are less brilliant than I?"
Only someone as poor as God—
that hideous Ouroboros of a man sucking his own dick,
forever brought down by the other-lovers of humanity,
who begot His only son with one of His creatures
the way man might splice himself with animals
(for 'man shares genes with worms',
genes being the promiscuous similitude
of summit and abyss) ...

only someone as poor as God
would accept the love of all equally.

Even if every sun must grow weary
of the fact that its light must shine *on* others
and never *on* itself—
even when it knows *it* is the source of what shines—
there are mature suns *who are shinier in their old age*
(because light *escapes* them like spender,
which they allure with their slippage),
suns that know how *to take a dive*.

Every mature sun
whose waste is the brilliance of sun-tanned spirits,
who must poison greater the weaker the atmosphere,
who can only be seen from below, darkened,
and who causes cancer in those who bask in him,
must learn the charming secret to their light,
the cruel humor of *what shines*.

The secret being
that what shines illuminates only images—
indeed, *the secret is only an image*.

92. The getting and the going from the get go

I represented transcendence for her
(especially being *the failure* they consider me to be),
something she couldn't have,
something beyond her,
what she knew not what to do with
and so couldn't get rid of.
She prevented herself from relating to me
as I am—
the void I continue to be—
from the very beginning,
since I was reproduced in the first place
as transcendence,
i.e., unmoved, goal-oriented, self-certain persistence.

She "wasn't sure
if she wanted to be with me
or if she wanted to be me."
Only one was possible then.
Now, neither.

I was just a physical being
that got in the way of her relating to an ideal—
she attempted both possibilities
by beating me to the point where I was not.

She saw my not-being-myself as a failure
and my movement away as a decline.
When a single feature diverged—
when my truthfulness went under
(disappeared beneath the surface, to *let* a lie appear)—
she reacted as if I had died
and she was dealing
with some new, strange, dangerous person
who stole something (a previous me) from her.

She couldn't be what she wasn't,
since she had to settle for being not-me,

and that led her, worst of all, to being what she was
and nothing but what she was,
lacking her absence.

93. Computers can't lose on purpose

I believe in a God
that maintains the illusion of being in control
with ease.

I believe in a God
that is a good escape artist.

I believe in a God
that swallows the key to his own cell
and says
"The prison is on the side of the bars I'm not on."

I believe in a God
that is still resting,
since it is still the 7th day.

I believe in a God
that doesn't intervene
since that would interfere with His own work.

I believe in a God that
beautifies simplicity with a chaotic world.

I believe in a God
that doesn't know how to use chopsticks,
that eats as if it's His first time.

I believe in a God
whose message is only preached by the Globetrotters,
and doesn't approve of Harlem
as the new hip spot.

Buy Me, Get Me Free

I believe in a God
that simultaneously does nothing
but accomplishes everything
and does everything but accomplishes nothing.

I believe in a God
that lets you bury Him in the sand
and give Him breasts.

I believe in a God
whose most successful pick-up line
is "I've taken shits the color of your eyes."

I believe in a God
that wants you honest,
whether your honesty is Mother Theresa
or Charles Manson.

I believe in a God
that hasn't made His mind up yet about you
but doesn't lead you on.

I believe in a God
that trips and falls
but turns in Skittles upon impact.

I believe in a God
that doesn't have a problem being only *my* God
but doesn't interfere with *your* God.

I believe in a God
that splits Xanax with a boxcutter.

I believe in a God
that cleans the bathrooms at a rest stop in South Carolina
and doesn't write dissertations on civil rights.

I believe in a God

that hides anagrams into local injury law firm commercials.

I believe in a God
with Satanic messages in His silence played backwards.

I believe in a God that loves His mother.

I believe in a God who lost His identity with His license
and no longer pays taxes.

I believe in a God that pulls a lover from behind your ear.

I believe in a God that carries around a tackle box
full of drugs.

I believe in a God that can sleep standing up.

I believe in a God that feigns modesty.

I believe in a God that rides His own inertia.

I believe in a God
that loses chess to the computer
to trick the computer.

94. My homeless homies

In D.C.,
the homeless shit
in the backseats of unlocked parked cars.

In Atlanta,
the homeless
ask kindly if you want to hit the crack pipe
after they take a hit in broad daylight
with the lighter you bummed them.

Buy Me, Get Me Free

In NOLA,
the homeless
bukkake Shinola onto your shoes
before you have time to agree
and shine them with their bare hands.

In Nashville,
the homeless congregate outside Hooters
in Hawaiian shirts
to watch the Super Bowl or the T & A
and claim to have jam sessions in the sewers
where Batman Returns was filmed.

I have a harder time claiming I'm better than them
than I do about young professionals.

95. When I write, what is said goes

If you rely on intertextuality,
you have nothing to say.
If there is nothing slowly killing you
and keeping you up at night,
then you have nothing to say.
If you have to accept apologies,
then you have nothing to say.
If you've never vomited in a public urinal,
then you have nothing to say.
If you've ever waited in line
to use the bathroom
or have sex
or buy tickets or sneakers,
then you have nothing to say.
If you've ever worried about transmission,
then you have nothing to say.
If you've ever shushed someone or clapped
in a movie theater,
then you have nothing to say.

Mass Merger

If you've ever judged someone,
including yourself,
on their own merits,
then you have nothing to say.
If you've ever claimed a right to something,
then you have nothing to say.
If you spill the beans
and turn the secret rule into an utterable Law,
then you have nothing to say.
If you sing karaoke
and you're not a desperate, old loner,
then you have nothing to say.
If you can't sit alone silently at a crowded bar
with your woes
without working, texting, ogling the bartender
or watching TV,
then you have nothing to say.
If you've ever been to a job fair
or donated to a campaign, project or blog,
then you have nothing to say.
If you're too chickenshit
and bank on slow annihilation by cigarette,
then you have nothing to say.

If you've ever laid on the floor in a public restroom
and embraced the toilet with your bare hands,
then you might have something so say.
If you've ever cheered on a cockroach
as it crawled out of your shower,
then you might have something to say.
If you've have existed little enough
to get away with revenge in this most secure of existences,
then you might have something to say.
If you've ever said "Aw shit, oh well" with a smile
at the free clinic as at an unhappy roll,
then you might have something to say.
If you've ever drank for free
out of half empty beer cans
and half empty cocktails after the ice has melted,

then you might have something to say.
If you've ever provoked a beating from your partner,
then you might have something to say.
If you've ever been cured
by the bleach and ammonia in a McDonald's hamburger,
then you might have something to say.
If you've ever said "No thanks"
to what the employers
or the women
or the blood-drivers
or the humanitarians are selling,
then you might have something to say.
If you've ever masturbated to cheating
and came when you got caught,
then you might have something to say.
If you've ever stopped up the toilet
the morning after a one-night stand
before sneaking out,
then you might have something to say.
If you've ever made prophetic remarks
and bent world to word through minuscule subtraction,
then you might have something to say.
If your life
is like a turd that didn't break when you flushed,
then you might have something to say.
If you've ever had to lie
because "Relationships are based on communication"
and because you were allowed no secrets,
not even the secret that you *are*,
then you might have something to say.
If you've ever given the illusion of productivity
but didn't conceal any time-wasting activity,
then you might have something to say.
If you've ever abstained
because you thought a prostitute might ask you
to rate her performance,
then you might have something to say.

You can never be certain you have something to say,

but when someone has nothing to say—
you just know.

96. Stomach cancer, maybe

Grid-locked traffic inside me.
The shit at a stand-still without any weight gain.
Motorcycle gangs riding the medians or the lines,
my farts.

Not the same amount going in
and coming out.
A worm or an X-Ray machine will kill me.
Foods not meant to be eaten together
causing simultaneous indigestion and diarrhea.
Making friends with my parasites
that are the real poets.

Not doing research on Web MD.
Maybe cancer,
maybe a worm,
maybe IBS,
maybe stress,
maybe booze or my diet.

Maybe a heightened awareness
that feels things that aren't meant to be felt.

Maybe a lack of bacteria or a lack of baseness.
Maybe too much acid
that's *eating me* and coming out in writing.

Her and I having this in common.
A metabolism so fast accumulation changes nothing.
Irritable enough to eschew world hunger
and engineer the future.
Shit as sharp as a dagger that pricks my finger.

Hepatitis C veins surfacing everywhere
because I couldn't keep my tongue to the mouth.

Same thing as Hitler or Kurt Cobain.
My body producing its own opioids
that fill my gut with rocks, making me delve deeper.
Quitting cigarettes potentially killing me faster.
Refusing insurance by refusing work
and carrying my pain like a parrot.
A wide open Russian landscape
throwing tigers at me from below.
The apple of my gut pierced by circus daggers
with my head intact.
My gut already dead and still peddling
like Jarry's bicyclist.
My intestines exploding like hollow-point bullets.

Life is too easy, otherwise.
Only the synchronous precariousness of the trapeze
is magical.

97. The diseases of the deceased do not desist

All the greats have been blessed by their diseases:
neurosyphilis,
irritable bowels,
AIDS,
megalomania,
seizures
or the disease of just being sick.

The worst have been ashamed of their diseases.

The best have the beauty that has consumed its 'flaws'.

Unsure if its blood or the beets in the bowl.
Taking pictures of the stool

Mass Merger

to show the doctor and your friends.
Your insides coming out with the food.
Can't afford to get the tests done,
but I have nothing to be sued for.
My intestinal health is giving me acne.
There really is nothing inside me,
just a floor model that isn't for sale.

Society purifying itself with antibiotics
and killing me along with the bacteria.
Then selling me probiotics,
insurance
and gym memberships.
Too much pain to hold the revolver steady—
they'll hook me up to a breathing machine.
My body will survive
and function better without me.
The cities will function automatically
and outlast civilization.

And only *statistical* accidents
occur within a 3-mile radius from home.

98. These women

These women *won't shut the fuck up about sex.*

These women make it easy for me to avoid them
with their passé excitement.

People have been fucking forever.
I can hardly think of anything less interesting.
God is even more interesting
than these message boards overflowing into the clubs
with the sexual code.
You could search the internet for their conversations
verbatim

and get exact results.

You get the idea we must no longer be sexual creatures
the way these women won't stop talking about it
and filling out surveys about it
and getting PhDs in it—
sex deader than God.

What killed God was God's integration into society,
when He became available to everyone
in the form of jewelry or bumper stickers—
when everyone got the stupid t shirt
(and even started saying 'got the t shirt').

I think you have a 7-year window tops
to get so excited about something that everyone develops.

People are fucking
like their genitalia have already fallen off.
We all missed the 'sexual revolution'
and yet these women can't shut up
about all the great sex
they are reading step-by-step how-to DIY manuals
to 'have'.

Everyone is fucking *as seen on TV*,
worshipping with stupid nursery rhymes.

'Hey, have you heard
about this new thing called breathing?'
Christ. I hope I don't give them any ideas.

This whole redundant craze of 'discovering your body'
with which the women are turning me off...
have they found it yet?

People are all carrying condoms,
so I carry ear plugs.

Mass Merger

Not to mention, men are fucking boring—
dicks are so boring
they've already been incorporated into everything:
toothbrushes, remote controls and skyscrapers.

Now that the women all want to be like men,
they are all becoming boring
and the only interesting ones
are unenthusiastic suicide cases.

Guess Bukowski closed the book with *Women*.
Talk about good timing.
Guess now I have to write about objects or deserts.

Everything else stinks of subjectivity
and politics
and the many
and all that shit these bitches are talking the fire out of
that I was doing when I was 17
only because I didn't know it yet.

LumpedIn:
Poems Unseduced By One Another

No more exile: integral trespassing.

99. Zoning out

"You can't get in *the* zone from your comfort zone."

But zoning issues only serve the government.

100. Flashbang news

The shit world has a talent
for always being better than it could be
and thus getting away with much
but only women could get an apology from the CDC.

Apparently, women's health issues
are offensive to the gender.

When I told X to stop drinking that time on Skype
when she was in France,
she chugged the Rosé,
had her episodic psychosis
and started burning herself with a Bic lighter.

"I've learned that burning yourself leaves no scars,
but hurts just as good as the blade."
She taught me so many things.

"Sex and the city"—
there's nothing about women in the title
and the show is true to the name.

I learned last night I can listen to Sweetheart of The Rodeo,
watch the republican national debate
with crazed subtitles
probably written by South Korean slave workers,
and read Roland Barthes's Image Music Text
at the same time.

I learned this morning I can turn my intense rants
(self-aware of their ridiculousness
even when they take themselves seriously)
into lighthearted art.

(Shit, I gave up the formula. I'm not supposed to do that.)

101. From the Everyman to the Anyman

I take care not to acquaint myself to any rules,
that I may forever have beginner's Luck
for anything that might unbeknownst to me
be a Game.

I float in this dead-man's ice bucket called the Party
like an alligator float
once the maddened anticipants have wet their rape whistles
with all the intoxicants they previously sank me with
and had to use to pump me up
to get out of me.

102. the sneakers of a dead man

> I have a knack for being subject
> to the phantasms your amputations project,
> and uncannily I may repeat
> what *accidentally* you *might* meet.
>
> Gave the same flowers as the abuser;
> my massaging hands becoming bruisers;
> with my freedom, acted out your Fate
> without needing you to calibrate.
>
> Whether acting or acted upon,
> we always come to expect the dawn;
> we base willing on that assumption
> and conclude self-knowledge with gumption.
>
> From the sudden appears the Event;
> then Reason comes when Fate already went.
> And "placing responsibility"
> is as suspect as humility.
>
> Only in collapse are we all in—
> only in decay do we strive to win.
> Only in radiance do we half-live,
> burned by the reception of the gift.
>
> Witticism is the sage's way
> when the lovers won't continue play.
> Mistakes are *what are already made*—
> produced, visible and under-played.
>
> The seducer forgets Seduction.
> The subject's germs taint the abduction.
> When the affinity seems elect,
> the donee is rendered circumspect.
>
> No one likes to lose, except to God.
> Commandments seem familiar, less than odd.

The accidental is a floating terror
because anything could be error.

Internalized blame and punishment
essentialize every accident.
And the Event is the fixity
whose presence demands remedy,

so that the imagination dulls
into a hyper-void that can pull
the body forward on its inertia,
repeating "I will never hurt'cha."

And so the apparatus that heals
becomes the Serpent that coils and steals,
constricting around the anomaly
until *the Corpse* becomes *Who* you see.

Entering the pit, you kicked up dirt,
and thought it causally dead, inert;
then, the altered pit became a trap
because *it met you* off the map.

Generally, all matters are alive,
intoxicating us with their vibe.
And we enter every room too late
to see the history of its state.

It *takes* effort to *become unglued*,
vomiting versus ingesting food—
playful *and* substantial, am I able?
Two sneakers hung from telephone cables!

103. Becoming and reversibility

Thought becomes a neurotoxin.
Absolute speed becomes total inertia.

Absolute mobility becomes total immobility.
The more you travel,
the greater the sense that you're going nowhere.
The harder you work, the less you get done.
The deeper you go, the more you find an absence of depth.

The disappearance of aesthetics
becomes the aesthetics of disappearance.

The destruction of experience
becomes the experience of destruction.

The artifice of reality
becomes the reality of artifice.

The subtraction of addition
becomes the addition of subtraction.

Absence presents itself
or presence takes leaves of absence.

For every temptation, there is a related way out.

104. Kill-time math

The conversion disorder of the DMV
whose dysplasiac speed defies the mental space
that becomes absorbed
in the courtly arrangements of chairs and receptacles,
into an eye-witness account
of the Supernatural efficacy
of this anti-Hell:

I counted 8 processing windows, three of which were closed.
Each row of stackable chairs held 14 persons,
and there were seven rows.

That's 98 persons ahead of me.
Each window took about 5-15 minutes
to process each person.
That's about 980 minutes.
Divided by 5 that's about 196 minutes of waiting.

With this kind of precision, I will wait forever—
that standard deviation of the miracle
in the fidgeting minds of people
coming into the middle of a process.

105. Joy-begetting joy

I didn't know it was President's Day.
Calendars aren't for stoners.

I wasn't stoned today,
and I didn't get off work for the holiday
because I don't have a job,
but I still didn't know what day it was
besides that it was Monday and that it was February.

Some of these holidays seem to float around dates anyhow.
Thanksgiving is the second Thursday of November
because dates don't matter to Americans
any more than Indians.
We don't exactly murder dates,
so we're not exactly responsible for forgetting them—
we just don't consider them.
We are inconsiderate people, temporally—
or at least I can say this of myself.
That's what happens when theory is put into practice:
history dissolves—
the future is dateless.

I went to Walmart
to *wander lonely as a cloud-based storage unit.*

LumpedIn

I kept seeing women too young to love
and didn't think much of it.
There are enough people anywhere
at any given time
to imagine that, like myself, the majority are unemployed.
But it was President's Day putting them in my life.

Finally, I stood at the whatever items or less line
behind some women too young to love
buying art supplies.
The black cashier smiled
at the little white girls with opportunities she never had.
I got up there with my stupid shopping list—
a box of Cheezits,
some gummy candy in the shape of the octopus,
(these were for to send to X)
some toothpaste and a thing of mouthwash.

"My grocery cart makes no sense," I said,
"I got the poison and the antidote."

She laughed a laugh
that interrupted the way she was standing there.
To some others, she was just octopus arms.
And there were enough others
to make her forget the laughter we shared.

It's shitty of me,
but I sometimes find it tranquil that life is shit in general—
that these simplest of kindnesses of which I am full
interrupt productivity with their appreciative influxes.
If there were nothing but joy,
I'd have nothing to add to the world.
(See, my morality needs the shit world.)

Absolute joy would be cultish, disgusting and suspicious.
It'd be *those* folks who'd get my shit side.

106. Flirting with disaster

My insurance agent is always so delightful,
making moves to cheat the system
and getting me imaginary deals.

She's a saboteur with the cutest voice
that sounds like sunshine being dunked
into a mini basketball hoop hanging on the bedroom door
of a future Kobe Bryant.

She is saving me money
by getting me discounts on auto insurance
with renter's insurance,
and I don't even pay rent.
(I don't even pay for my insurance.)

She is potentially saving my life.
She speaks to me like she knows me,
and I don't get upset about it
like black women do sometimes on the train.

She shows me what it's like to be admired from afar.
I bet others don't talk to her like I talk to her—
like she's my soulmate
about whom I have to do nothing
since that's just the way it is.

She could be a hideous beast
and her living conditions could be shit
because she sleeps in her own path of destruction.

But I would never know that
because she is a sweet angel to me,
precocious in her lovely tonality.

There are anti-capitalists
who would boil her on the steps of Congress.
I think about cutting them end to end

and trying them on.
Of course, they don't want you
to actually walk in their shoes—
those freedom freaks that don't understand Elvis metaphors.

Shit, she has me writing a poem that's sponsored content.

That's how beautiful things have become.

(But don't call me a bourgeoisie…)

107. How to be single?!

The women industry has made a feel-good movie
to make being alone bearable.

The single-morality
couldn't have come from anywhere else
but people who can't bear themselves
or who become their own mothers—

but shit, it ain't called "The Art of Being Single."

It's called "The Single Manual."

It's a step program—a fucking pyramid scheme.

What's the first step?
Probably "Never leave your friend's side."

Step two?
Probably "Mingle, never go home alone."

I'll tell you what though,
there's nothing "single" about the singularity
that *I* am.

108. No ultimatums

What I like about volumes of poetry
is that I can never have a favorite.
Poems aren't intrusive and don't interfere with one another.

I guess it would be the same if I had volumes of women,
or guns
or cars.
I could never choose a favorite then.

Maybe I only choose favorites
because my tastes are so refined
that the vinegar-flavored women of my sensitive palette
don't come along often.

But who am I kidding,
I gamble them away
and get ahead of myself when I find women like that.

How could you not be feeling your Luck
with a woman like that?

Or maybe I only choose favorites
because there aren't many women
who would put up with me in the first place
I'm always talking murder
terrorism
and all things 'negative'
on the first date.

Anything to not be vulnerable
to answering that question *women* always ask:

"What's your favorite ___?"

109. The Easter-egg basket

> I hide all the eggs
> to prevent myself from putting them in one basket.
>
> In other news,
> the sniper laser on my forehead makes me a dot-head
> or is my third eye.

110. The Law of Poetry

> Her feminist role-model—
> philosophy PhD and JD—
> told her she approves of dating poets.
>
> I'm only a poet like a duck is a duck.
>
> I'm only a poet like an anti-poet,
> but I think both are stupid.
>
> She liked to eat ass, so I figured:
> "A lawyer, I might need one of those one day."
>
> Anyway, what could a lawyer have to do with the Law?
>
> Being a lawyer or a poet
> is like being a middle man that's already been cut out—
> like a C-section baby.
> Bikini models are getting those,
> what could the harm be?
>
> Like any inoculation,
> it turned out to be just a little prick,
> over before it began.
>
> And she's still hemmed up
> in all the Bureaucracy involved

in that give or take one-year stint.

111. She butt-dialed me

X called me last night, didn't say anything.

I was the butt she ate.
She was the butt that dialed me.

It's almost Mardi Gras.
Some guy's erection
probably dialed me from her back pocket.

I wonder if she still uses the data-hoard phone
that I smashed before I left.

But I think she was on the other end of the line.

Usually, when people butt dial you
the other end of the line is the sheer chaos of bodies
moving inside clothing with pockets.

But there was 37 seconds of silence on her end
to me saying "X? Helloooo?" before hanging up casually.

It was a unilateral call.

She was testing me.
She was always testing me.
When she beat on my head after I confessed my sins,
when I cheated on her in our 'open' relationship,
she was just testing the microphone.

I must've sounded so stupid.
That same naïve inflection.
I'm a female protagonist in a Cassavetes film.
A sort of girlish eagerness We all love

that comes from an absent-minded attentiveness.

Unusually non-random thoughts.
I bite my arm and smell the skin.
My mouth always made her vagina smell bad.
She always picked up the tab, and I always offered to.
She never apologized.

This call that is a silent sign:

My clownish tears that don't bother the government
with unsellable repossessions.
The Will? What's that?
Flashes of wit like UFOs that are just camera smudges
and tediously detailed vignettes.
Commercials where the woman is shampooing her hair to
orgasm.

112. A lover's logic

Maybe she was testing what it would feel like
to hear my voice again
and didn't say anything, *but said nothing*,
because my voice brought up no feelings.

Maybe she had it on speaker phone
while she was fucking the better man
and "came super hard" when she heard my voice.
He certainly is too absent
to not let her do some shit like that.

Maybe she was checking to see if I had the same number
so she could give it to the lawyers.

Ah shit, whatever.

113. The silenced phone call

> Maybe she just wanted to show herself
> in her presence only—without any content,
> without a message, like God.
>
> Maybe her myth needed silence
> to convey itself one last time and resist death.
>
> Maybe it was this open-ended Form
> that was a call to me,
> the myth-reader and –maker.
>
> She was there on the other end
> and didn't need to say it for me to know it.
>
> Only she could make the phone line
> into a tautological form,
> yet spiritualized and not automated.
>
> Maybe she froze or panicked
> and fled.
>
> She let me experience that fear.
> She was always honest like that to me.
>
> Maybe she didn't know what she was doing.
>
> Maybe God doesn't know what He is doing!
>
> Maybe you can scare God away with your magic
> that gets over things more quickly than cause-effect,
> also.
>
> Maybe God's that honest.

114. Unnoticeable notifications

I worry that my free time is killing me
because the scientists are trying to trick me
into believing that inactivity is deadly.

In my free time, death whispers secrets
that come out wrong on the page.

I have experienced spans of time
larger than retirees
whose days are longer than mine.

I'm going to die of colorectal cancer in a few years
from sitting so much
like a king.

My death has given me
the space to extend my powers
into a future I am skeptical of.

What exhausts you,
energies me
and vice versa.

I could be this alone here,
or at Machu Picchu during the off season.

I can spit out truth like sunflower seed shells,
and swallow the edible part
of the concepts I collude with.

I can travel the world
in less than 80 days
and have the rest of the 120 days
for Sodom.

I am the Dr. Doolittle of objects.

115. X, X, X

X dug my grave but forgot to put me in it.

Now, I'm looking at that empty grave
like the hood of a car
with a rebuilt motor waiting to be installed,
like a stackable container,
like a Ziploc bag fresh from the box,
like the plush duckling her toy fox terrier gutted
yet still played with,
since its toothless mouth couldn't destroy the rest of it.

X put me in the ice-filled bathtub,
but forgot to take an organ out.

Now I'm looking at that ice-filled tub
like a sports magician who believes in sports medicine,
like an iced-over lake
everyone but me is afraid to walk across,
like the butcher's savory counter
that doesn't even smell of meat or salt.

X put antifreeze in the desserts but forgot to measure.

She let her love get the best of her trappings—

like a cryptozoologist.

116. 'Missed' encounters

There was another of them at the supermarket the other day.

I saw her from across the store.
I continued shopping.
I no longer saw her and headed to check out.
She pulled out right in front of me from a secret aisle.

LumpedIn

She was standing in the longest line,
but she had skin like me and nice eyebrows
and wet, curly hair,
even though it was thirty degrees outside,
so I figured I'd wait.

The line didn't move, so I creeped over to the short line.
There was no cashier in her line.
The manager came over to point her to the shortest line.
She noticed that I snuck over and made a comment.
Then, she invited me to get behind her
in the shortest line.
She courteously put her items
on the he conveyor belt, rapidly,
so I could put the divider down
and put my items on the conveyor belt.

When she noticed I had a few items in my cart
and that the conveyor belt was full,
she scrambled to rearrange her items
to give me room.

Little destinies like these
that pop up and disappear ecologically
like microscopic organisms—
these encounters that cannot be missed.
They are too dismal and humorous—
universes crunched before they bang.
Can't lean on them, must lean into their disappearance.

It's possible that the 'real' me has already *come and gone*—
not that that has mattered, since I am still doing things.

I'm living in the post-me world
of an 'I' that *me*anders beyond **something whatsoever**.

I used to imagine I'd already finished my life's work at 27.
There was nothing more to do.
I arrived at where the magic begins—

my disappearing act behind a light
coming from such a distance it freezes existence to a delay
and gives the impression
of linking up to other disappearances
in a constellation of the future.

I encountered a new world—
passing from interesting to fascinating—
one populated by new peoples,
who see that I am an object that already served its purpose.
A fascinatingly useless object,
carrying itself like a stoned, bobble-headed camera—
held by a cameraman powered by whiskey
yet able to surgically remove erupting innards of depth
at all times.

People that bear no resemblance to X,
individuals without closure
who don't construct a personality
out of the lack of material for one,
who just leave that lack be—
truly distant creatures committing ambiguous crimes
that haven't been made punishable yet.

The kind of simple people I simply cannot love
above daily life.

117. Eviction notice

Do people notice anymore?

How could she accept her God's love
if she couldn't accept mine?
Am I that bad?
Am I a total dead end on the path to divine love?
Does my flesh curtain over the barbed-wire fence of the
Beyond?

LumpedIn

Is my body not sublime decay?
Is my ambiguity not unlimited and tactile?
Does my Destiny not curve my Destination
to an involuted, involuntary summit of myself?
Is my appetite not curbed by an inviolate cavity?
Does my chest not *beat itself* unlike a gorilla?
Does my heart not pound on the door to itself that no one answers
with the urgency of a woman escaping a predator?

Do people notice anymore?

Do they notice others?
Do they notice themselves?

Do they notice the telescoping pores in the Styrofoam ceilings?
Do they notice that the minute hand
slightly regresses before each tick?
Do they notice the freckles
ascending impossibly up the vertical bridge of the nose
like mountain goats licking salt?
Do they notice that the handprints on the windows
don't affect the way the light passes through?
Do they notice the way people sometimes mutter to themselves
what the other is saying, as he says it,
like ventriloquist dummies?
Do they notice that peeking into some people's lives,
waiting like they do,
is like peering into a microwave
rotating and sucking the fluid out of food?
Do they notice the reverse-pedophilia of children?
Do they notice their own magical disappearing act?
Do they notice the similarities
between hospitals, airports, malls or a blank slate?

Has a video game ever made you weep?
Have you forgiven yourself yet?

Do you have the corpuscularity of a vehicle?
Do you dream of the shelves in the supermarket toppling
end to end
like dominoes in an integrated circuit?
Have you ever wept at the wondrous vacuity of your own
creations?
Have you seen yourself *anywhere* in 5, 10, 20 years?
Have you seen your reflection in a screensaver?
Have you given your nightmares the free space they need
to tell you nothing?

118. Creeping it lovely, and eerily meaningfully so

I'm going to break your back
with all the luggage of my love
that I'm going to ask you
to help me carry.

I want you to gore me
by giving me the better half of the deal
and pull my intestines out
like a magician's colorful, endless rope
and stick all the leftover organs
inside you.

119. You *would*

You *would* expect me to write poems in your absence,
that aren't about you—
lapses of poems that confusedly
can't put their finger on *it*
without you to barricade their youthful, polished
dissatisfaction
with your diaphanous body-shield
like a wall that pushes back

and collapses when they stop beating their heads against it.

You *would* let my career ruin
so that in the ruination it only attracts Muses
who pity this loss to poetry—
making miscarriaged poems that I never knew.
Then, I too will have to flee.
And you know how much I hate that.

120. *Smokey the Bear* and book-rentals

When you live at home, you must clean up *after yourself.*

This *after*—is it the *after* of the *after-party*
or of *after tomorrow* (the *after* of a future you)?
Is it the *after* of *after you're dead*?

Is it the *after*— "I'm *after* her"—of pursuit?
Or is it the *after*— "You *take after* your father"—
of inheritance?

You must run ahead of yourself
and, not looking back, leave nothing behind (not you).

Or you must remain behind yourself
and in your janitorial arts become the clutter.

Smokey the Bear says
only I can prevent my fire from becoming a forest fire
(by cleaning up *after myself* and going home).

I'm allowed my fire,
but I must leave the forest how I found it:
with a pre-existing fire pit.

I can *use* the fire provided by the wood
whose existence is ensured by the park rangers

who 'keep the forest alive'.
But I can't *create* a fire—
and the forest never disagrees
on this point made by its spokesmen.

121. Ack, you STD

Be careful not to accuse someone of saying Nothing,
because the Nothingness they most likely *really did* utter
has crept into your accusation
as the object of the declaration.

And, once again, the object takes its revenge.

Whereas the accused has an Allie in the object,
there is something fearful about uttering Nothing
to an accuser.

122. All sign

You can never know if someone ever *really* loved you.
Love is all sign.

You're taking insignificant gestures not meant for you seriously
and running with them to the end.

There's no integral calculus.

I'm always treating it like a computerized detonator,
pressing buttons with anonymous functions,
cutting wires without linking the colors to a function.

I have to admit, so far, I don't qualify for the bomb squad,
and like I said, if you hand me the detonator,

I might press it out of curiosity.
I'm attracted to the way modern constructions
go down vertically
and absorb their own rubble,
when the biggest of things go the way of computer files.

If we're going to be together,
I wouldn't trust me with any of the responsibility.
I can be the hero, though, accidentally,
if you're patient.

I can become a once-in-a-lifetime experience
at any moment
in my vertical, isolated collapse
so perfect it seems to defy gravity, its only support.

123. Memory is an abject phenomenon

I gave away all the things she gave to me.
The gift is never healthy
when it begins to accumulate value.
The gift put back into circulation
frees up the magic of a quasi-mystical mourning
that returns with the conspicuous absence
of spiritedly abject memories.

I gave her gifts to the people she hated me loving.
And it felt glorious.

Without any artifacts to dull my senses
with a nullifying familiarity,
the unaltered memories of her
leave depth behind in their welling-up.
With her disappearance,
there is no reason for her not to show up
metonymously,
according to whatever chance gesture of appearances.

Buy Me, Get Me Free

And there is nothing stopping her absence,
that trails me from an unnoticeable distance,
from altering my trajectories with my curious dejecta—
the collusiveness that spirals magnetically
around an elusiveness I'm minimally aware of.

The "once-in-a-lifetime"
can follow you down every avenue
with an interpersonal patience that avoids startling you.

You cannot measure yourself against lost history—
but the memories detached from concrete entities
can smother you with soft-tissued love.

She hoarded all the pieces of me—
the values of which hardened and formed exoskeletons
around their ghostly machinations—
not to cherish or mourn them,
but to nullify them into an equivalence
with the rest of the objects in her little apartment
that were images without concrete form.

My letters, my clothes,
my annotated copies of Philosophy in the Bedroom,
Elective Affinities
and The Collected Works of Rimbaud,
the boxcutter I gave her on our first date
to split her Xanax with
and the box I put it in
wrapped in excerpts of Nietzsche shitting on feminism
that were torn from the textbook
of the Feminist Political Philosophy class we shared—
indifferent alongside unopened boxes of paper clips,
the silverware in her drawers,
the dried dog shit
that's been hiding under her bed for months,
the stuffed animals from immature flings,
the expired poison underneath her sink,

LumpedIn

the cigarette butts that the Acid rain of New Orleans
has beaten into the infertile top soil
and the cardboard cut-out of Elvis
hanging its flattened head
with a dispassionate crease in the neck.

Objects controlled, and yet unmastered,
by their unimaginative, dead-eyed contiguity.

Collectively,
and especially with the vituperative aid
of virtual technology,
we indifferentiate the past
with a circumspection that freezes both past and present.

The past never resurfaces,
because the present never occurs.

Equality destroys diversity
and we never settle back into ourselves—
thinking we never settled for less.

The Natives understood this
with their unflagging self-understanding
that heightened with their destruction
by those who knew not how to appreciate
and who couldn't tell themselves
from the cultures they murdered.

The Natives understood diversity
and hated being photographs—
since photographs freeze the soul
(the specificity of the singular
into the indifference between moments.)

The paparazzi are trying to make you
as indifferent as they are to themselves,
as if they have no language,
to freeze you into a life-less, asymbolic cut-out,

to steal your fatal relation.

She murdered me with proximity and exposure,
whereas I sacrificed her—
so that I might continue to respect her
and harness the powers she fears.

She told me the disease has made her feel unattractive
and she no longer takes pictures of herself—

she might just have a chance…

124. new new

Romance is supposed to offer a love experience.
Lies were realistic before,
but now are self-referential fantasies.

The need for knowing
forgets of the other absence, in gift relations,
that preserves a social distance—
the fatal.

The need for knowing focuses on the visible
and preserves meaning
by reproducing the saying, lawfully.

Communication is a compulsive distraction,
and jobs are new forms of entertainment
for those who stay at home.

We would violate the Universe to a cold fright,
only to prevent the potency of an eclipse of force.

The invisible is more useful,
acceptable,
when it is measured with tedium by cameras

and then cut.

The absence of life can be edited,
unmasked,
like a newfound corpse—
the social as open-casket funeral
where a smile is necessary.

You can love something simply because it exists now,
fascinated by the void reasons used to fill
as thought's fate.

125. Military time isn't cut in half

I always find myself logging on from time to time
because that's the world.
I don't expect to find anything,
but I'm not "not looking for anything."

I never get excited or disappointed
when browsing the inventory.
The ocean has this effect on me
that art destroys with its politics.
I don't have to ask questions:
the simulacrum is there in full—
nothing to add to it,
nothing it subtracts from some nature or another.
The ocean reflects the sky superficially
without being illuminated.
I speak neither,
without my breath being taken,
at the horizontal liquidation of both.

I search for *profiles*,
but the profiles are all ruined by personality.
I'm looking for someone who *is* the profile,
who isn't reflected by the profile.

I don't want the referent.
The past is real, I don't want reality.

I don't want you.
I want the profile, the "not you."

Her profile said to message her if you like trash,
so I messaged the profile.

"Trash Humpers?" I said.

But the profile's response was interrupted by her.

The thing about glass houses is that, like opportunities,
if you don't blow them today
you're forced to exist in full view.

126. Death in the objects of consciousness

When you still overflow with childish wellness
and are in the habit of paranoid, accepted solitude
against all-natural odds
and have the *continuous* imagination
of an omniscient victim
that drops aptitude into ineptitude,
like Jerry into Tom—
every object around you
becomes a potential, fully realized murder weapon.

The children, some of them, dream not of defense—
but of accidental, unprecedented
and thus wholly unpunishable murder.

The household objects surrounding your little form
are the stuff of violent bashings
and operatic tortures and vivisections—
from the elaborate and gratuitous mechanisms

of Dominoes that link up to imaginary machines,
to simple body horror at the hands of gum balls.

Home Alone is a perfect myth of
the child's gratuitous anxieties and death wishes—
approved by the State.
In the myth, thugs are so desperate
and poverty is so insane that two hardened men are reduced
to a child's isolated entertainment.

As we get older, this childish wonder of murder
is destroyed by facts:

in fact, with chemicals, not only objects,
but foods, surfaces and air become weapons without users.

And how could one call murder
the misuse of an object
(become a weapon, a function)
when death, in the form of a single message,
is the very essence all products
(including the air, which was produced by God)?

So, you get used early on
(by the taboo that distinguishes use and misuse)
to dying slowly yourself,
outnumbered as you always are
by those inertial condensations of labor—
that robber of death that is Death itself.

127. Little shit poet

Today I'm a young poet, whatever that means—
this poem says so
(I don't argue with poems over words).

It's never what I say,

but the way I say it that upsets.

Sometimes, though, my heart bottoms out
and the suspension of judgment breaks.

Only I do what is customary
and go buy a new one—used.

If I am naïve enough,
never worrying about effects or truth or value,
I can be struck down
to a size you might regularly see or artistically despise—
whatever your *persuasion*—
when one of the girls on the Bachelor says "piggy pigs."

Everything I do is original to me,
so I never verify what I do
or this statement of which the scrutiny is even questionable.

I never pretended to be convincing,
but no more so do I pretend not to be.

128. Dim sum poetry

The carts come by with ambiguous meats
and dishes the waiters cannot explain.

You have to eye-ball everything
and it is impossible to tell
whether the same dishes come by again or not
upon further visits.

There is no guestimating
how the Pinyin scribbled down on a Yahtzee scorecard
will add up to a cost by the end.

Nothing could be further from Western dining,

whose actions are only valued
in their consequences.

129. Medium of the Medium

My poems are energy.
A material, tangible energy.
The gap between the screen and my typing is intangible.
I try to type faster than the computer
and catch the computer when it's naïve
and absent from itself—
that's where the poetry begins.
Or else the poetry is when the computer beats me
and types faster than I do.
It is wary of doing so with me always suspecting it.

Rather, it's all part of a code,
an unearthed secret turned monstrous.
My code, the code of the medium—
I'm the medium of the medium, sometimes.

I'm writing on an older generation tablet that's a few years
old, completely obsolete—conspicuous and retro.

It's cracked, but intact.
I have a way of attracting cracked glass that doesn't break.
The windshield of my 1986 Beemer cracked
from a lighter exploding
that had been rendered invisible by little nook in the dash.
The crack completely split the windshield in half,
but it remained functional.
I liked the crack, but my car guy said I better replace it
because it could cave at any moment.
Shit, I'd been going 100 down Georgian highways
full of rock-throwing haulers, no problem.
But I caved and replaced the windshield.

Buy Me, Get Me Free

I was moving to New Orleans.
It's like Jumanji over there.
The earth just eats and craps on your vehicle.
They don't have any car washes over there
because of the futility.
The debris makes driving invisible, a guessing game.

So, they set the windshield
they got off some retired version of my car.
It's about a 7-hour drive to New Orleans from Atlanta
if you steadily drive 90.
I'm not sure when or how,
but by the time I was there the crack had returned,
in a different place and with a different style.
It came up from the hood directly in the center
and looked even more dangerous and appealing.
The Beemer wouldn't let me
'steal' its accidents and glory scars.

I couldn't change the Beemer
and I couldn't change X or myself.

130. New or Lean (Codeine/Meat)

She decided to take me to Dirty White Lenin Party.
Unlike the Red Lenin Party,
this is when rich people wear all white
and booze through art galleries opened to the streets.
The opening of the galleries into the streets
represents that every day is art
(that is the marketing campaign for NOLA tourism)—
but the fact that there are still galleries
shows that the 'everydayness' of this art
is only a party that sells the inebriants that sustain it.
This was after we met up with one of her law-school
friends—
the one she told I said was ugly—

LumpedIn

at one of the Uptown bars close to her school and
apartment.
She told her well-informed friend
I wasn't a feminist but had my reasons
and my reasons weren't typical.

I felt a demand for explanation coming,
so I exploited her moral courteousness,
pretended to be busy by talking to the bartender.

But then the bartender went outside for a smoke.
I followed him.
I let the girls set each other's brains on fire
with their industry speak.
I was just getting in the way of their Progress, anyway.
Joe, the 47-year-old black man,
had a laugh incompatible with the laughter of discomfort.
"There is no slavery," I thought, "for the time being."
I handed him one and lit one and told him to extend his
break.
By the time our shots were dead-on the shit,
after we exchanged numbers
and planned on playing jazz together,
X's friend was properly entertained
and that cab had arrived.

I sat in the front of the cab,
which I don't enjoy because Uber's branded itself,
like everything else, as the personable cab company.
All the cab drivers are licensed psychotherapists,
and they are encouraged to mingle with the customers.
Luckily, X is outgoing.
Otherwise, the silence would've potentially exploded the
engine
and cut the brake lines.
Not afraid madness might break out in silence
so much as afraid of losing touch with reality,
we keep this infinite conversation going.

Buy Me, Get Me Free

I don't like talking to the driver.
Last time I did,
they asked where the four of us were coming from,
so I told him "We just filmed a porn
called 'Three Guys, A Girl & A Pizza Place'."
I miss the Russian immigrants
who were physicists or composers over there
and who you knew blamelessly hated you.
They were honest.
They never thought the silence was awkward.
They brought the nukes and the tigers with them
in their Siberian silence.
They were putting their kids through the Ivy Leagues
and weren't saying shit.
Now, everything is "such a pleasure" for the workers
I started saying "You're welcome" in place of "Thank you."
Don't people understand I contribute to the economy
in my consumption
more than some people do in productivity and taxes.
It's hard, dirty work—
with all the interactions and surveys.

We arrived in the shit part of New Orleans
where the tourists are.
I had to buy the password to the bathroom
at the coffee shop we got out at.
They wouldn't keep the bottled water
I had to purchase to piss,
even though I told them I didn't want it, just had to piss.

We made it to White Lenin Party,
where the art galleries
were throwing up white people into the streets
dressed like posh, socially acceptable and concerned Klu Kluxers.
I had to buy craft beer from a street vendor.
The only good thing about New Orleans
was paying a dollar for Dixie Beer,
the beer they told me to finish with, never start with,

the beer responsible for cleaning up Katrina,
when they partnered with FEMA
and started bottling it with all that water.
That beer had all the fire of para-military,
the inertia of a whole community,
the black people that zig-zagged through high-caliber firing-squads with 72" TVs on their shoulders
and Sean Penn in his relatable dingy.
That beer kept me company like the better man
and the bum I kept seeing with five dogs without leashes
who never looked back at me.

I dropped the craft beer
on one of the famous streets with lots of foot traffic,
picked it up and drank it.
X was afraid I'd contract something.
That's just because she and everyone else in this place
believe this place bleeds debauchery.
Luckily, the Dixie had me immunized.
I had already befriended
the magical filth obstructed by this voodoo politics
these residential tourists are proving themselves to
while proving it to themselves.

There are too many people here.
It's like the Fun Bully turned the city upside down
and shook all the people from its pockets.
Here they all are, rolling like pennies on flat surfaces
until they fall flat—
the loudest part of the process.
There are so many people in existence
that two-thirds could *fail to procreate*
and the population would still grow.

The people here don't flatter the booze
into making them look stupid.
They make the booze itself look stupid.
Fucking nihilists.

Buy Me, Get Me Free

I had to take a break on Bourbon
and sit with my woes and smoke.
She made me read this Bukowski poem
about getting a blowjob to be able to keep loving your
girlfriend.
She told me about the guy she was fucking before me,
about how insecure he was
and how she told him to read Bukowski
because I was into Bukowski and because I was tough.
I was too drunk to read it—
but I stared at her phone for a readerly duration.
And because I didn't read it,
she couldn't ruin it by association.
Buk and I have it like that.

We went into a bar
and when I pulled out my card to get our drinks,
the bartender said "Cash only, faggot."
I apologized and pulled out $9
because I was already breaking twenties too fast.
"$17, faggot."
I apologized and gave him the twenty
because I didn't want to wait for change.

X and I stood outside a place without space to sit.
We ended up arguing.

I said Mike Tyson is the greatest.
He had to be restrained after knockouts
or he'd start eating the downed man.
That was before brains had surge protectors,
when what they plugged into you
might catch them with your explosion,
when the crowd couldn't clap off your fire.

Nevertheless, it's one more Dixie Beer
and I can love her again.

131. God *in* my life

God is the myth of my life.

Everything happened, nothing has occurred in my life.

My life is an arrival—with a long wait—
at a scene in which there is nothing to see,
that I endured only to see something.
The lack of the visible in this visitation
mythically doesn't disappoint.

God has no more meaning than my life—
precisely why my life is everywhere.

The moments have been, at best, unreal.
That is the wonder and the fury.

All sign, my life is this lovely non-event.
That with little reason not to run into itself eventually,
has little reason not to run—
like a loosened thread
that exposes the magical expensiveness
of the material behind and within the former cloak.

132. The local and the transistent

Another—*an other*—is not Other.
It is completely legible, preferred (not transferred)
and local.

The global—the exclusion of the Other—
is wedded to the local
(that mythical transcendence
that misses its mark all the better
to conjure up a *novel* nostalgia),

This is the same as the exclusion of the Other
for the sake of *One Another*.

Locally sourced revenue is a ravine—
that or a Vine, which is clipped.

Here, contingently, only kudzu can save us—

an invasive species *we* introduce.

And introductions are far from seductions.

And because our insistence
lacks consistency,
what we need is an unfamiliar word:
transistence.

This new form of 'approach'
is never lacking in what it is not.

Not to mention, this transistence—
when put on mute, it's nonetheless transmuted.

133. Out-dated, time out-doing itself

Simulation does not mean "fake it to make it."
That's the slogan of production.

It's more complicated than that.

Lie and wish and hope for an accident
and maybe get the truth.
That's the pray and spray mentality
of the Thompson machinegun, i.e., of WW2.

Simulation is more than truth emerging out of falsehood.

LumpedIn

There is never any cause-effect relationship at all.
The lie *is not a lie*.
The truth that 'follows', however, is still true.
The truth exists in its fully achieved form
from the beginning,
unhampered by history or narrative.

134. Googley eyes turned inward, false consciousness and thought

I don't have the time to think about the possibility
that my mind auto-corrects my thoughts.

But there are people, according to the psychologists,
whose stream of consciousness is disrupted
by metonymous thoughts automatically.

My thought flows like hyperlinks on Wikipedia
taking me from former lovers
to the person who abbreviated barbecue to BBQ.

The fruits of my thoughts
are those mismatching themselves on the slots
that also give the impression
of a secret attraction to each other
and to the gambler.

And that is another problem altogether.

Some are fascinated by it.
Some want to kill me—the dreamer.

Because the dreams that I dream
might interrupt the dreams of a cloud-based collectivity,
whether mainstream or alternative.

135. The blues are disappearing again

The birds are cracking skulls with themselves
in my window again.

It makes me wonder about people
who can be infuriated by these sorts of 'impositions'.

There are people terrified of insects
like they were raised on Mars
and never developed indifference.
I, on the other hand, was a child once
and performed vivisection on all those tiny animals,
peeling off the under-bark of softened logs
and watching some creatures scatter
and others ignore me,
underestimating my stature and seeing my form
as a compensatory darkness to that of the bark.

I admire the cockroaches living in a world of petty giants,
scattering away with half their guts missing
and with their missing legs stuck to wings
that, although they are for show
(according to me, the viewer),
can still kill the cockroach
if their functionlessness doesn't function.

The red bird's knocking himself out to prove he's strong,
so he can get it in.
I'm worried he won't have the energy to fuck.
Happens to me sometimes.
(Why I don't compete for affection,
not even against myself, i.e., for glory's sake…)

The strong ones don't do this,
but they too are insufficient alone.
They knock each other to prove who's stronger.
They're lacking in-themselves—
needing others to overcome to become what they are.

LumpedIn

The women have them souring their juices
with all that competitive edge—
but women get the strong one no matter what,
it's their way,
so they're not worried.

The one at my window can't lose to himself.
His victory may or may not be guaranteed
(he's a fucking bird;
I'm not sure ornithologists will confirm or disconfirm this).
His image cannot leave the game to beat him at his own.

Anyway,

the red bird is back again—
so you know what that means: Spring is coming back;
we are all making comebacks
and no longer beating against ourselves like the bird
with holidays of responsibility
(New Year's hasn't ended yet; Lent is almost here).

The blues will soon be last year's man—
and no one pays attention to bygone headlines
(wrinkles are the only headlines—
wisdom makes your forehead melt down into your eyes
so you can't be emasculated any longer by the newspaper).

The sundresses will be recommissioned
and I will be dressing for sweat again.

Depression will no longer have concrete form—
and the passive anger will return in the heat exhaustion.
It's too cold to get angry now.
The cold simulates anxiety and saps your energy.

The depression is a shored-up energy necessary to endure,
like the conspicuous fury of the para-suicidal red bird.

Those ice caps are starting to melt

and we are not yet ready to take the responsibility
or to enjoy the beach-front property we are about to inherit
from the destruction of a former world.

I will forget about the depression soon—
warm weather makes me naïve
and careless mistakes keep me cool.

But, even though it's still freezing,
I think I'll leave the bird
to that Henry Rollins mirror-punching shit
and go run errands or something.

136. Vegan-rexic

Her nail-thin body scratched me.
To her body, I was a chalkboard
with "I will not talk during lecture" repeated all over it
like signatures on a cast.

Her body was screaming at me like she tended to.

Her body said:
"There are plenty of things to eat,
but nothing to nourish me, including you."

I think that's how I developed an imagination
that brought bacon and donuts into the boudoir.

Her philosophy in the bedroom was starving her.

137. Reality

The men were committing perjury
and added a digital signature

that never changes from document to document
when they made Woman *all sign*,

so the women disappeared,
which they have never had trouble doing,
into Reality.

Men (including many women)
fucked up the Revolution.

138. Japanese 69

69 a girl with an hourglass figure
and it's like going back in time.

139. DP (Director of Photography)

If men had female bodies,
they would all be getting dp'ed—
knowing that they could.

So why aren't all women just constantly getting dp'ed?

They have been educated that they can?

But women withhold secrets beyond passion,
that go beyond *multiplying dicks*.
That's what you want to believe.

Technically, if pleasure was so great,
women would *multiply dicks* to infinity.

Multiplying dicks has never been more streamlined.
They are all attached to heteroflexible mentalities
that wouldn't mind the experience points.

Buy Me, Get Me Free

There's no morality preventing this from happening.
Those days are over.

Neither does it have anything to do with nature,
for if nature leaves room for drives and desires,
and decides who has more holes,
then we would expect women
to fill themselves from ever entrance like parking lots.

But women still have something
for powerful men to teach them,
and so know unwittingly the brilliant artifice
of inexperience—
with which they make dicks disappear.

140. Bourbon

On the rocks, I drink it before the ice melts.
I dump the ice out and start over.

I want the cooling property
isolated in and taken from the ice
without the watery essence.
Plastic cooling cubes would be nice.
Of course, plastic ice cubes would have to be re-cooled,
whereas I can just toss the regular ice cubes.

Neat, I only like to shoot it.
The warmth is too crisp to sip.
It goes down and I motorboat big-titted air
like Mr. Ed laughing at the ease and superfluousness
of human life.
I begin the night with socially responsible cheers
as the glasses hit like bumper-cars—if I must—
then, with a neat Tourette's I embellish with a flimsy tongue
and a whistle-less exhale.

141. Losing it again

I'm always losing things.
And the angrier I get about losing something,
the more likely I am to lose something else
even more necessary.

Today, I needed to cash a check.
They don't come often—
so I love going to the bank
since I only go to get cash, never to deposit it.

I put the check in my inside
coat pocket at some point.
Checked it several times before *heading out…*

142. Nietzsche's head

Bataille kept Nietzsche's head staked
to a coatrack screwed to the floor in his hotel room.
Nietzsche's head looked queer
as someone who had their death mask
made in their twenties—
whose death mask wouldn't fit on their thoughtless head.
Chocolate candies shaped like poker chips
of varying, disorganized values
came out of the eye sockets
like receipts returned via the suction-based elevators
at the drive through of the bank.
Bataille volunteered to be beheaded
because Nietzsche always appeared to mock his sensitivity.

Inside Bataille's Nietzsche's head,
Nietzsche was always scratching at his own chalkboard
to get the attention of his students—
the drives.

Buy Me, Get Me Free

The drives took turns presenting found-objects,
and each was teacher for a day.

To punish the out-of-line ones,
Bataille's Nietzsche had them write on the chalkboard
indefinite amounts of times,
never using the same words twice—

unlike our teachers
who behead with solitarily-confined mantras
written highly arranged amounts of times.

143. Target

I like to go to the suburban Target at 7ish on Sunday
when all the riff-raff non-white poor people have time to go,
making Target no longer an alternative
to the riff-raff-non-white-poor-people at Walmart.

It is a quieter time.
The white people are not there to silence their youngins,
and the riff raff children are easily excitable
without pocket devices.

The people here are like me.
They wander through this downed space station
looking confused like world leaders,
like they are walking through an anti-art art museum
or a butterfly garden on a grey planet
with other grey creatures conveniently called aliens.

I never notice things missing from the shelf
or whether things are arranged wrong.

The white people are not here.
And there is an unsilenceable quietness
between these people

LumpedIn

    probably thinking the same things I am:
    that this place is more expensive
    and more underused
    than the Walmart next door to it,
    and that life is shit
    and has a way of giving you peace after you flush it.

    But it leaves streaks that are not primordial.

144. When the bathroom becomes a restroom

    I sit on a heated toilet
    and my shit never looked more flakey.

    The expensive toilet paper rubs off on me
    as my shit disappears.

145. A personal life

    I have to be my own personal assistant,
    life coach,
    psychoanalyst,
    hygienist,
    stylist,
    trainer,
    chef,
    dietician,
    shopper,
    editor,
    public relations rep
    and promoter.

    I have to do all the menial tasks
    involved in making myself live.

They want me to pick my questions,
my responses,
my poison,
my slavery
and their brains.

They want my life to be a choose-your-own adventure novel
that I have to write as I read.

All that button-up tedium of a bottom-up consciousness.

I get all the glory but have to do all the work—
that's not glorious.

A pill to choose for me—
how many lifetimes wasted in a laboratory
are required to get me this?
We know the lab techs are as plentiful as the albino mice,
anyways.

146. The shit-taker

They all would ask me
the same question:
"Ariel, why'd you take all that shit?"

"You took all that shit from her
and you lost your fire.
You had many opportunities to get out
and you didn't take them.
Why'd you do it?"

"She was playing you.
She loved you, but she was crazy and mean.
She was fucking guys
uglier and less interesting than you.
Her friends all sucked

and she had no soul, just information.
Her tits were fucking big
and the hair was lasered off in all the right places
and she'd let you do anything you wanted to her
and she was rich
and she was going to get richer.
But she was %100 horrible.
Why'd you do it, Ariel,
why'd you put your fire out with her?
Why'd you build that fire
just to let that smoothskin piss it out?"

Maybe it was the money,
maybe the sex,
maybe not.

I always just told them:
"I was doing what most of us are doing,
I was a kid poking a dead body with a stick
to see if it would respond.
That's all."
The body never speaks for itself
in death.

147. When the landing sticks you

I consumed her.
I was what people call an 'empath' for once.
But I didn't feel sorry for her.
She dug her own shithole
and the stress from the effort
stopped her up too bad to empty herself in it.

A shithole-digging slave really only wins
if he or she leaves the job emptied of the indigestible matter.

I just felt what she felt.

Buy Me, Get Me Free

She was a nervous wreck.
I became a nervous wreck.
I started having panic-attack-induced orgasms.
Because they had such shit sex for so long,
some women are resorting
to no longer pretending they want to have it
yet still doing it anyway
with an even more intense compulsion
and even learn to get off on their disinterest.
Sex is one thing you don't have to be 'into'
for it to make you cum—
a little microcosm of bare life.

Resentment towards the 'into' that vanished
in some cases led to rape fantasies.
Others just jumped on the bandwagon,
so they never had to be 'into' sex.
She took little enough care of herself for neither of us.
I got hemmed up in it.
I knew what I was doing.

I used to ask the black cashiers
at the Circle K a block from our place in New Orleans
where I bought her Marlboros and her Ben & Jerry's
what they would do in my situation
(not interested in following it or anything).
All those black women told me not to put up with all the shit
or take any of the blame,
but I always thought they only believe that
because they don't have time to waste.
I was unemployed and paid for by my abuser
so I had all the time in the world,
and the insanity was a luxury I could afford.
I never wanted to invest my time,
just spend it.

I wouldn't take any of the blame.
I owe myself nothing,

not because I deserve nothing,
but I'll still take some of the glory.
I got out of there without any bruises or internal bleeding
because I know how to lose.
If you jump off the bull too early you might get gored—
the bull is an endurance game
whose art is the dismount.

Who am I kidding? It wasn't even a hunch—
I got lucky, that's all.
I don't need to learn a lesson to get lucky.
Fortune is never trying to lecture me.
When it fails it doesn't scold,
never makes its failures my problem
like she did.

I guess I made it out
like someone who survives a fatal accident
because they weren't wearing their seatbelt
and got thrown from the scene.
Fortune is the world's counter-gift
to humanity's detachment.

148. Chic Fil'A

The objet petit á
or Chic Fil'A—
same thing!

The 15-year-olds
inoculate the sandwiches
with their cult-like enthusiasm.

I'm the leader of a cult here as I eat,
and I drink the lemonade first
before any of my worshippers
(I'm a bad leader).

Buy Me, Get Me Free

God's work is too yummy to wait on
(that is, to use to lead by example).

Yet if the Church closed on Sundays,
maybe I'd want to go more often.

149. Cluster-fuck ATL

    The buildings here don't communicate
    or look at one another
    like people at a family reunion
    who've have never met most of the people there.

    Neither habituated to each other's presence,
    nor surprised by it.

    They don't even look
    at their own reflections coming off one another.

    They cannot be rehabilitated,
    so this situation shouldn't be deplored.

    They have a shy 'look'—
    but you find this untrustworthiness a challenge.

    They disappoint you
    to keep their personal space impersonal.

    They are your best friends who disappear without notice—
    who you never try to contact
    because by the time you think to
    you forget again.

    Seeing your reflection in them
    is like suddenly being recognized by an Alzheimer's patient
    who will forget you again.

LumpedIn

They blow your hair back
when you walk through their doors
that let everyone in without touching anyone,
and it falls right back into place.

150. Simulacrum/desert

Fake tits protrude, don't hang,
from a body
like urinals from sectioned bathroom walls.

Plastic surgery is too caught up
in literal semantics.
The parts are implanted—
too much interiority.
They have a recovery time.
You can't just grab them and go.

My heart drops
like snack cakes out of vending machines—
just read the key and enter the code.

But bodily plastics will become detachable and
multiplicitous.
Small tits at work
and big tits at the club
and no tits at home.
A body no longer constrained to the interiority of its signs.
Put on your running legs—
for real this time!

Or why stop at bodies?
Save your personality to a data disk
and plug into whatever personalized form,
prefabbed to be inhabited
by whatever looks like a personality.

Buy Me, Get Me Free

Today, be an alarm clock radio.
Tomorrow, a Woman.
Then, why not an Idea on Wednesday?
A body personality or a calendar—
why should there be a difference between them?

Isn't that what the Internet is for—
free use, free connotability, freedom from creativity?
The unfree react to the obvious unavailability of creativity
in the omnipresence of models by becoming models,
by modeling themselves on themselves,
by grafting themselves onto themselves,
by taking themselves for all they've got,
taking themselves for inspiration
and for comparative literature,
by the free use and free connotability
of bodies that process themselves
for lack of creative process.

I have taken to watching porn
in which hard-bodied, cut men
fuck monstrously obese women.

There's something about the juxtaposition
of a totally Hyperreal bodily stature
and an indignant body
that constantly weeps itself and plays itself where it lies.

A male body that is no less deep
in its hugging of itself via skinniness.
A female body that is as insubstantial as ever
in its outward projection—
with an anti-matter
that corresponds to its girth.
A body that surrounds itself like a halo—
a body that is two bodies
(like Plato said the original beings were)
and the space between them.
A body that escapes itself

to be embraced by itself.
A body that consumes itself
and expands on its own devices.

151. None of the proceeds from this poem will go anywhere

> Someone is getting a $10,000,000 book deal.
> Someone is carving a tag into a bathroom stall
> of a condemned building.
>
> Someone is getting a PhD.
> Someone is getting an MRI.
> Someone has more RBI's than W2's.
> Someone has tight abs that IBD makes firmer.
>
> Someone unearthed an alternate universe
> after the rain loosened the earth.
> Someone is writing about the Grand Canyon,
> doing Kegel exercises.
> Someone added too much acid to the Beeker.
> Someone found a dead body and didn't rat.
>
> Someone graduated with honors.
> Someone is plugging their butt
> with graduating circumferences,
> preparing for anatomically-correct anal.
>
> Someone is stealing material
> and getting away with it via cryptomnesia.
> Someone is 'before their time'
> and dying too early.
> Someone liked the sequel better.
>
> Someone owns all the cars Evil Knievel jumped.
> Someone just sold an unread Harry Potter novel
> for an undisclosed sum.
> Someone lost a lot of money at the pawn

for the "Collector's Edition."

Someone has all the time in the world
in a floppy disk from 1991 labeled "Vanessa Williams vs. Cher."
Someone just passed from being a waste of time
to being a hazardous waste of time.

Someone is drinking out of a bottle
shaped like a gun.
Someone is betting on politics
and winning more than voters.
Someone is squeezing the last drop
of a bloody, watery mixture
from a rag in Guantanamo.

152. I'll still be here, don't worry

The innocence of the suburbs
is an ominous mobility.
Nothing is built with an eye towards the future.
The clouds here are like abductees
ducking and rolling
out of the white van God tossed them in
somewhere they wouldn't recognize.
Eternity ends (or is dismissed)
as soon as the sarcophagus is opened.
The houses here will not last.
They are not designed to be lived in.
Like a car depreciates as soon as you drive it off the lot,
the house rapidly ages
as soon as you walk in the front door.
The houses are like the forests,
as soon as you walk into them, all the life hides
and suspends itself until you leave.
Adults cannot see Santa here
and families cannot see the magic of their life-proof houses

they are preventing from occurring
with their presence.
This place would be easily abandoned
if there weren't constant work that needed to be done
on the houses thrown together like movie sets—
if the built-in obsolescence
didn't provide Hispanics, who no one ever offers cervezas,
a steady stream of jobs.
This place could sustain itself
if everyone here got jobs repairing each other's houses.
But if all the jobs left
and all the houses collapsed in on themselves,
this place wouldn't really look much different.
Maybe they are saving all the nukes
to drop on these agoraphobic shopping malls
called suburbs
when they stop supporting themselves.
Everywhere here is an outdoor fallout shelter.
Americans forgot about the nukes
as quickly as they forgive and forget about one another.
When the nukes are dropped
as cost-effective means
for clearing all the unproductive avenues,
afterwards,
they will just fly planes over that drop liquid asphalt—
like the planes they put out wildfires with.

You will still be able to find me there,
sitting, frozen in the middle of some other complaint
like the Pompeian everyday-lifers.

Hopefully, they don't catch me like my zipper
during masturbation.

153. the dingy

if there were a beyond

of language, then there
would either be nothing
or something.

if there isn't, there is not
even nothing.

nothing is only another sort
of depth and beyond.

154. The Departure Depots (Deposed)

I already know the value of *any* action;
and this knowledge is inconsequential.

The result of *any* action is the same—
accidentally the same.

The end recycled by the means

From this point on, or still,
nowhere.

I could go nowhere anywhere.

January 2016

Samurais without katanas can still disappear.

Planets no longer align, only the bars on slot machines.

I am testing the extent to which the world needs me—its patience. Or the extent to which it will produce what I have singled-handedly produced but haven't shared. Unless the sharing with a small group of patrons is enough to have what I have made lose its remote flavor as what refuses to be wrested from its origin. Unless merely creating them is enough for the world to fold its distance and cut me out as the middle man. I know that the world will reply "No. I have made a life of my own with someone else." I am hated the way only someone who has been loved is. I play its worldly game and it doesn't beat me on at least this move: the unemployable wastage of my powers that are greater than those in need of them, those who demand that I take advantage of my talents (the ones they lack but desire).

I wonder what it's like to live in the dimension at which large women make themselves look thin simply by positioning themselves at such and such an angle.

When ugly women learn their angles and intermittently succeed in capturing some beauty of themselves, they learn seduction. When beautiful women discover that their best angles are lacking and scarcely fail at capturing some ugliness in them, they unlearn their seductiveness, and it grows accordingly.

Aversizing (The Science of Repulsive Advertising). They say not to expose your pearl among pigs, but you can volumize your cloying pig-eye—now clam with tongue in cheek—with Tampax Pearl.

When one we revere does something that lowers our opinion of them, for instance, when they are intimate with someone base, we never forgive them if we originally respected them like a worthy adversary. They have seemingly not only made a bad move but have ruined the game for us to the extent that we no longer wish to play with them. To quit is only another move. Yet to imagine ourselves without the game is no mere move, but another game.

I embarrassed her when I slept with that shopgirl at American Apparel. She embarrassed me with an immature revenge: she did the same thing I did—and nothing is baser than an undifferentiated, entropic, lukewarm revenge! Revenge should be cold, exotic—a revenge that does not lack its victim! Eye-for-an-eye—what a banal approach (and without the humor of the insignificant). And had I still thought her my equal—the lack of creativity would have hurt more. Her argument: she would have been more artful had her opinion of me not dropped as fully as her half-eaten heart into the acid of her stomach once I was seduced.

I felt her pulse most certainly when the sulcus of my penis congested her esophagus like Charmin that decomposes more slowly because of its useless thickness. Her skin liked to hide that she had a heartbeat. My body can tell time and send and receive pulsion with an immediacy that is less revolutionary than functions on an Apple Watch. I sometimes gave her vibrating alerts when I wanted to be touched—and even then, the phantom vibrations were when she checked me most enthusiastically (or compulsively).

January 2016

The more perspectives we take on Nothing,
the less perspectives Nothing vitally takes from us.

When you count on your fingers, the space between fingers becomes like the 'pelvic' space that separates the leg-parts from the torso-part on Barbie dolls—like sexualized objects lacking genitalia.

I like vaginas smooth as mirrors dusted with cocaine, that are closer to Nothing, to a lack of a lack—perfected by denegation, like America—than to a sex. But there is another type of vagina that is like the intestinal limbs of a fallen tree encroaching through a broken window. And that has the dangerousness of a wound!

When the ground falls into the depths and a chasm juts horizontally, superficiality becomes dangerous—and low. Superficiality deepens and loses some of its fresh air. But above superficiality as such there rises nothing. And nothing thankfully cannot deepen.

There is something—the Nothing—that not even nothing can be said about, that allies with its image with too much ease, that is too insignificant to not exist, that persists like nothing else because it is the where—the other where, where else—of the nothing that has no need for you, that cannot be resisted because it puts nothing forward, because it exists before we do, ahead of us, beyond the forward movement of time, and because it also follows us and—slower than us—erases our tracks. Away from nowhere and towards nowhere, what a modern, spherical conception of time.

We've run out of pleasurable organs—as a result of organization:
Clitoral orgasm: Christ (Superficial Organ)
Vaginal Orgasm: French Revolution (Mediate Organ)
Cervical Orgasm: Industrial Revolution (Depth Organ)
Throat Orgasm(?): Integral Reality (Demand Organ)

An escalator is a *flight* of stairs—undermining of the object.

My moments are larger than usual and take more energy to be folded for the sake of traveling through. My memory is not bad—my moments are too singular and enduring to be remembered. Woe to revolutionary moments, for they are short, flashy, easily bent, easily reduced in duration (not durable)—speedily traveled through, or rushed.

It isn't too soon to write a female character who shows up drunk to a party without knowing she has cum all over her face. That's what politics is.

Sitting too much, the scientists are warning us, can kill you. Either sitting is trying to rob you of a natural death or the scientists are trying to steal your death, that was to come from sitting—death by leisure. Sitting and I would not be as alluring if there wasn't the potential for death at any moment because the potency of death would be lacking. You see me slowly killing myself (or rather, disappearing) and yet not aging like a sloth, sitting—as ignorant of dying as a cat curled atop the backrest—and you won't admit that your dicey eyes roll to a favorable numeric configuration, when even luck is beneath me. Or your indifference defers my death, my throw, my roll.

How perverse are people who are not ticklish? You either are ticklish and you pretend not to be, or you aren't ticklish and you pretend to be—tickled by your own pretense. Lacking ticklishness is like lacking a birthday—as only a clone identical with (and thus absent to) itself would.

"There are more physically attractive women than there are physically attractive men." Doesn't this mean there are more unattractive women than there are unattractive men? Nothing less attractive, nothing more suspicious than dating down. This is only forgivable in those whose attractiveness is so great that the chance of dating horizontally is significantly low.

In love as in masturbation, grasping makes blind.

There is often a mutual silence between friends who've spent much time together that is either an expression of luxury and respect or an expression of neutrality and derision. In the first case, only what is worth saying is said, but not every thought worth saying is said. In the second, only what is said is worth saying—every thought worth saying is exhausted in speech. There is something disgusting about the thoughtful whose thoughts lack distance between speech and themselves—this proximate silence is something like the fact that if the physical mechanisms below and behind thought were communicated in thought, thought itself would occur only awkwardly, if it could ever arrive at all.

Thought itself is that which skips steps—whose belated arrival is, when you think about it, earlier than it should be. If it is on time, it's because its "too late" is produced by its "too early," and vice versa. Thought—that revolutionary wastage—lacks the history necessary for dialectical sublation. It is a kind of impotence—a weakness that must be embellished in seduction.

Thoughtful—like a child blowing bubbles with soapy substance that doesn't clean, who pops the biggest and the littlest with the same cruel enthusiasm.

New Year's Day Parade from the comfort of my own home. Who goes to events? What kind of experience-obsessed mongoloid goes to see things live in person? It was intended to be watched on a screen. Therefore, I get the original version on the screen. The real version has the secondary character of a dying medium 'alive' only in its absorption into the medium that surpasses it. But the real lacks the spirituality of the dying initiate cannibalized in a sacrifice. We don't consume it—out of lack of respect.

He cut himself open and let his guts drape to the floor like spaghetti while on LSD, when a friend told him "There is a child in all of us that comes out on LSD." Taking words for reality is a euphoric psychosis.

The *shitty* hues of entrails are incompatible with the irradiated hues of high definition.

Words flow into one another like tree branches—some spiraling around others and touching them or others first, some dying, some obscured by their own growth; these conspiring, these complicit, these not touching or being touched; some closer to the ground and requiring more effort to reach the canopy; some closer to the canopy, innocent in their ease. The former sturdier, the latter lighter and more fragile. Each the profane of the other. Some have an accompanying destiny, some are destined to get in the way—two destinies, each also the destiny of the other destiny.

The profane in language is to me like a great piece of media that overloads your circuits, the energy of whose message you circulate and repeat to dampen its signal. Profane speech is like listening to a record that you love to the point of mere repetition, recycling, the point of no return, of farce, of its becoming an indifferent form, of a challenge to the artist to die—or a zombie's enjoyment of the electric plastic of brains. Think of the game hot potato.

There is a space of neutrality of life to death and death to life in the frozen food section. One thinks of frozen sperm banks—suspended life—and people's heads frozen before they 'die'—suspended death.

January 2016

No miracle of life, no miracle of death—there is a matter-of-factness about frozen food, Walt Disney's frozen head and frozen cum that is disturbingly exact. In that case, life is disturbingly complicit to its production. Whereas in the past we were disturbed by life's complicity to its destruction. Or even worse than that, when what disturbed us was its continued existence after its destruction (the Holocaust). Now, we are astonished at its continued existence after its technological achievement.

Soon, virtual technology—the term "virtual reality" is still absurd and abusive—will be integrated into healthcare. There are already virtual pets to comfort seniors 'anxious about death and the after-death.' When well-being becomes objective, the subjective element will over-compensate. Intravenous virtuality (which exists metaphorically already) to dominate in a victim order. A bunch of goblins smug in their perfect virtual reality, when shit rolls backwards up a hill like cars are known to do up certain hills in neutral. The smug survival of the defunct in its virtual, mail-order perfection—something to think about.

The up-to-date is no longer—even before this sentence ends. If you reached the end of the previous sentence, you missed it—the update.

Whenever I imagine Baudrillard, I imagine a little man who hides his greatness—like an Indian—with the subtlety of a hibernating computer that functions doing background tasks. I imagine him as the good cop, who is always the evilest when it comes to accomplishing the job (fait accompli). We are driving away after dropping off the duffle bag. "Wait. What happened to the grenades, J.B.?" I ask. I look over. J.B. remains silent, smiles a weak smile, holds up a finger from which three safety-pins dangle. "One always arrives at one's ends by a mixture of objective chance and weakness."

    That some fool withholds the power to mock me doesn't make me wrong about you. You're more precious than you think, more singular—almost too singular, like me. That I enjoy myself in you doesn't mean I'm wrong. Your exhaustion from the up-to-date communication of your rep accompanied your forgetting rank ordering. Which came first, the exhaustion or the forgetting?

My truths can be singular, too. They self-destruct when subjected to intensive, rigorous interpretation. I should hope that my loyal little truths would not respond to interrogating torture and give over to an indiscriminate, histrionic confession of secrets. I should hope that under the pressure to spill their guts, they would tell only what is wanted—information, simulacra of the form 'information'.

"Well then, what do you wish to know?" Nothing about this question qualifies that knowledge, the thing wished for, will be granted in whatever statement that follows. Not only that, it doesn't say anything whatsoever about (and makes no pretensions to) reality—so it resists any claim against its feminine simplicity. Whoever claims to have taken the cookie from the jar is the worst player—they end the game by realizing it.

Truth is a dancer
who grinds in your lap,
who you're not allowed to touch
and whose vision, that of a pro,
says that all you will get off
on is your own assumption.

I either have herpes or I don't. If I have it, then I could gain a pleasant distance between myself and the morality of sex. On the other hand, if I have herpes and I know I have it, I'm not supposed to have sex with disease-free people without a speech about the facts of my invisible, symptomless condition. If I get tested and have herpes, my sex life will be enforceably research-based and truthful. Sex will have an added compulsory dimension that it didn't need. Compelled—forced to need. I don't want to know if I have herpes, and if people can be sure every day they're not going to die, someone will still sleep with me for the candor of my uncertainty.

January 2016

Precaution and pre-cum are incompatible. The former, when powerful enough, neutralizes the latter. The latter, when cunning enough, ignores the former as if precaution were a rude child.

I find it comforting that time travel hasn't been invented yet, and that reverse time travel is theoretically impossible. If time travel existed, someone could skip my life. If anyone is going to skip my life, it's going to be me. If time travel existed, I'd have to move faster than docile speed, I'd have to skip my own life to make sure no one else skipped it. There is something distasteful about being (actively or passively?) skipped by the foreign, the only former flavor of which being that it previously had no relation to you.

My face is all body. My face is considered nudity. That also means that, because all body is face (and a whole body is too much to have look at you; hence the nudity effect), my face is twofold. It previously was locked in a dual gaze with an opponent. Now, it is its own exponent. Only Medusa before me, and some women here and there, knew of this inversion—to my knowledge.

"I'm nowhere but here," he said when he deactivated his profile. That could be translated "I am nowhere, but I'm still present." In the context provided, it could be translated "I exist only in one place at one time at the risk of inhabiting nowhere." Either way, it amounts to an existence so uncertain of itself that it must include the totality of what it is not in a simple statement designating its position. I'd rather just be nowhere.

She was interested in me. My interest in her had slightly declined when I saw the monstrous body of the guy she was seeing, who she had no shortage of complaints about—him being a chronic video-gamer. He was fat, with unattractive face, with hair the open-casket, funereal arts of which reminds one of the over-farmed, exhausted California mainland seen from the passenger side of a rental. Balding—the immutable terrorism of a pattern. But then she told me, addressing me by my first name, that they rekindled some old, dying and indifferent-to-death feelings for one another in Arizona—that other favorite squatting ground of UFO enthusiasts. My interest disappeared. Something abducted it.

"I'm a smart, intelligent woman." Representation is taxing… Obvious secret of America.

She decided that my biggest fear was 'to be just anybody', to get caught up in a general equivalence, which is worse than being nobody. It is no wonder she cheated on me with someone average name "Joe." Luckily, I made it out as nobody, since she couldn't make me anybody else.

2016. The polar bears of the San Diego zoo, frozen by camera-friendly glass, got "winter-wonderland-style" snow donated to their media room by the public and Coca Cola.

Still today, every limp handshake makes me think of a limp dick on a shower, not a grower.

No one ever concerns themselves with the good that may come from some atrocity. They fear a perfectly honest evil person.

Human scenery. The Truman show was perverse—there is something monstrous about the enormous effort it took to achieve what must be so simple for the world: to seduce a man into believing in the reality of his existence. The hyper-masculine perversion of seduction in the technical perfection of special effects.
    But the world of The Truman Show still has order: everything is staged. The only one who believes in the reality of Truman's situation is Truman. The exotic is eliminated in favor of a coded

universe—the Truman Show—with only one message: Truman. But the exotic universe and the banal universe were still what they were.

Disorder: a scenario in which a city is designed to streamline social encounters; a whole city, a *real* city, designed by observers to observe and catalogue the totality of encounters; a city that functions like any other city whose development was 'spontaneous and natural', a city whose reality can be contested by neither its inhabitants nor its visitors—so real that it came with its own infrastructural complaints, its own *scene*, its own irony, its own banality, perhaps even built-in alienation, anomie and anomaly (for only a form as empty as any city can continue to 'embody'—that term secreted from the mucous membranes of the materialists, as slick as the city—the reincarnated, already-dead sociological spirit).

This enormous testing ground whose data expresses nothing due to the chaos allowed to enter the laboratory. This observatory/city whose understanding is lost to its exactitude (the complexity of models—this *reality effect* given to models—reduplicates the original problem, and if anything, this exactitude of science, that reproduces its problems in its models according to a *non-intrusive* circularity and reversion, provides a perfect alibi for science).

There need be no city of this kind. The cities already in existence function this way unintentionally. But one can imagine a king who related to his kingdom as a form of entertainment, who curiously observed the happenings in his marketplace and narrated puff-pieces to himself, whispering wide-eyed obscenities like golf commentators—human scenery.

If you go to another city, you sometimes get the impression people notice that you don't belong there. Cities can be like excitable media, the disturbances of which alter the mental tonality of inhabitants. In your own city, people seem look at you differently, like they know that you inhabit it. Why are we more seductive elsewhere, beyond our city, when precisely *our* city is filled with strangers? All cities are the same. All the people in all the cities are all the same. What prevents me from a traveler's seductiveness in my own city?

Buy Me, Get Me Free

If self-administered torture were the wagon-wheel of science—animals would make very bad subjects. Humans, on the other hand, would cure cancer with a stupidity they have been well-prepared for. Let's hope this doesn't happen, not for the sake of the human beings involved, but for the sake of a future humanity who might find again in its diseases worthy adversaries.

When you cum on a woman's glasses, you only ruin her sight. But when you cum in her eyes, you ruin her makeup—and that is worse.

Roll our eyes when every dead-serious, disinterested anchorwoman pushes feminism's political correctness and mutual masturbation to the point of mutual blindness (the way love is blind, i.e., indiscriminate)—because this is easy. But discriminating *against feminism*—this second-order discrimination is made almost impossible. And with good fortune! No one protests protestors—the protestors have ruined that potential for the continuity of protestation by showing how ugly they are, how what makes them ugly is the protestation itself. Who still accuses accusers?!

Enjoying a victory given to you by an opponent is a greater sign of defeat than defeat—it expresses the insignificance of the trophy. We are passing/have passed from an order of losers who played the game without believing in it to an order of winners who believe in the game even when they aren't playing it—and the opponent is laughing at us.

The good thing about morality is that the formation of morality signals the death of its object, the death of the thing systematized signaled by its very systematization. The bad thing about morality is that its persistence corresponds to the suspension of the death of its object.

January 2016

Women may one day discover after it's too late the absurdity of 'their discourse' in the fact that no one would ever take "masculinism" seriously. The newly discovered history of women as the second history of History, the recycling of History—what is liberated most of all is an entire retrospective of scholarly gruntwork. The Humanities love feminism for the service-providing service it does them (it allows them to be of further service).

If the masculine is that which determines meaning by producing -isms (to the point of the man calling his discharge jism), then the -ism of -ism-giving is absurd. But if the feminine is what absorbs all -isms and destroys meaning, then the -ism of -ism absorption, as absurd as it is, will destroy itself and all theoretical edifices no one else believes in with it. So, long live feminism!

One day, we will pity the billions of sperm discriminated against by the egg. At the same time, we will hold the successful sperm accountable for its success.

The further liberation of the female orgasm in the form of medical information and pornography together with the further emergence of *femina contemplativa*. But wouldn't a woman who didn't believe in the 'female' orgasm be tried as a witch?

The offended, hateful look on the moral psych. professor's face when a student advisee declines the shirt that he offers. The unthinkable rejection of the Good—transparency of Evil.

The best professor I ever had—great feigner of the most eloquent speech, plump enough for the oven, brilliant, hospital-wall skin, cute as an animal that can easily kill you, sweet as antifreeze. The best professor I ever had—not well-bred (father in the army, mother a bookkeeper), stylish as a beauty who understands embellishments, always cheery, all-too-cheery, always short and secretive, whose characteristic laughter made her writing readable. The best professor I ever had—immense spirit that gave me hope for, to destroy my faith in, the spirit-killing strap-on-athon of academic philosophy. The best professor I ever had—leading researcher in her field, whose unintrusive reading of him opened and limited mine. The best professor I ever had—leading researcher in her field and still associate professor.

Philosophy—where I had free-reign over the women. A conservative Republican Christian and an atheist anarchist in the same class—feminist political philosophy. I seduced where truth reigns—a wolf in sheep's clothing.

There is a city in which, to prevent littering, all residents were asked to leave, and around which a boundary was erected to keep them out. The preservation of the planet and our departure from it, together at last.

Is there an unrequited self-love?

Baudrillard wrote Forget Foucault, so I forgot him. I never even read Forget Foucault.

The Bible Belt ties off America at the elbow. Florida, the forearm, falls limp into a lukewarm body of water. The narcosis that extends through the body keeps California—habitat of the other Disney— from drifting off into that colder, darker water.

Pisces. The shit that piles above the water is the smelliest if you keep your head above it.

Life is an exit strategy too. From what? For some, the inconspicuousness of death—for whom, in turn, the horror of life becomes invisibility. The beauty of life is always elsewhere, in the

January 2016

eyes of another form. For others, life takes on the singular quality of death, which unbinds and unwinds, and is saved from the brutality of any other form.

Cupid is sometimes wrong, and sometimes misses his mark. When Cupid misses, there is disorder. When I am in love, I can never be sure if I was not hit by an arrow intended for another target. One is always subject to Cupid's hastiness and occasional lack of form—his shortage of arrows notwithstanding.

Death is not like this, having never been wrong. Death alone is casual—never early, never late. In the end, death alone gets you—the perfect partner to save you from yourself. A surface that absorbs but does not reflect, that, unreflective, cannot destroy the perfection of a face uncertain about itself.

I always hope to relate to my best ideas like a tube relates to toothpaste—completely incapable of internalizing them once they escape.

My epiphanies often slip away from me before I can recite them. They flee like easily excited women from those who move too quickly. I hasten to forget them so they don't become *more astounding* precisely in their inaccessibility. They could have fled because they feared me—and any idea too weak for me should not be mine.

Truth, that deer in headlights—language frozen in fear and fascination.

What is so repulsive about zoos is not that Nature is subject to us, but that Nature is complicit with us. There is a pleasure in the resurfacing memory of Nature—a stroke of wit on the part of Nature—when the animals' violence breaks through their cuddly ruses. This nostalgic pleasure erupts with what it perceives to be the irruption of repressed, honest cruelty into an artificially tame order—or an artificial break from its natural laziness and indifference. Part of what repels us from the complicity of Nature to our models is that we react by siding with Nature's indifferent wrath against us, interpreting that as love.

Because she has nothing left to give, she gives nothing to her lovers. Because she gets nothing out of it, she takes everything from them.

Only for humanity are the perfect as hard to stomach in their perfection as the monstrous are in their monstrosity. Sure, but so long as there is still a distance between perfect and monstrous, both are at least bearable. You must either love someone who is monstrous or someone who is perfect, loving monstrosity in one and perfection in another. If you love someone who is both monstrous and perfect, you risk both fearing the uncertainty about which is behind (or is produced by) what action and losing respect for each in the interactivity of both. Self-love is included in this.

It was the absence of autonomous extremities previously grounding and freeing the body from its center of gravity that gave Apollo's torso its demanding look. *Whatever form concentrates also demands from you the interactivity it previously had amongst it's now severed organs.*

There is a lack of intrusiveness that comes from the familiar, whose peaceable banality does not need to be monitored, giving you the distance necessary for thought. There is in whatever streams indifferently from the monitor a schooling in inattentiveness that is necessary for thought to appear in the negative space between multiple tasks.

There comes from the insignificance and secretiveness of some beautiful person (whose beauty, we think, demands recognition) an attempt to make them signify at all costs the injustice that remains in our system of recognition. In reality, as we know, the insignificance is more troubling than the beauty. No one fears beauty anymore.

The cost of ignorance is solitude. The cost of recognition is resemblance. While both lack use-value, which is acceptable, the former lacks exchange-value, making it impossible to accept. The proletarians of beauty make themselves ugly because they cannot accept being used for their beauty—like the slave who exalted his soul because he got his body on loan. A similar attempt to make the passive appear active. Their fatal mistake: they 'make themselves ugly' *to be recognized.*

Self-contempt becomes tolerable only in the contemptible once you have learned the hard way that no one trusts the self-contempt of the admirable. But only if, that is, the diagnostician dares to tell the simulator that *he isn't really sick.* Fear of being wrong and a principle of uncertainty are two entirely different matters altogether.

Akrasia. Attempting to prove an absurd truth, one perishes absurdly. Attempting to prove a self-evident truth, one perishes redundantly. Alienation from lack, ecstasy from excess. Whatever the Marxists thought about the mental waste of the best and brightest, about *what good use* all that mental effort could have been put to, we can imagine the destructive tidal wave of intelligence—which combs over the mental landscape like a glacier whose size masks its movement and speed and might have hid beyond the oceanic horizon, had thought not dissipated into repetitively weak waves.

The current vogue of eliminating "micro-aggressions" through mass-sterilization (or speech therapy) that corresponds to the ineliminable aggressiveness of the species—how similar is this to the aging obsession with sterilization that formerly corresponded to the philosophical liberation of death. When immortal death no longer came from above, from God, but from below, from microbes—the *ground*, on which round-backed animals (Kafka) could not turn over, remained a source of insecurity. On our knees praying or on our hands and knees scrubbing. But if one scrubs harder what one cannot see, the scrub will wear more quickly—the obvious wearing-out of the hygienic apparatus against the invisible (or uncertain) disappearance of the germ.

The total recall of the profile against the momentousness of someone beautiful. One observes the profile pictures get uglier the moment one views them. One observes the descriptions get dumber the moment one reads them. One observes these in the character referred to here, Ariel Samuel Ackrum, as well, provided one still believes in reference.

There are people whose belief in reference was once so strong that they even believed in the 'ironic distance' they exchanged for its improbability.

What redundant people hope to find in online dating are those who are alone *because* they are special, rare cases, as opposed to those whose being 'single' makes them common. The greatest pleasure of the redundant person is the self-imposed redundancy of those unexchangeable, accursed ones who eliminate their suggestive power to enter exchange.

For every relationship in which we hoped to pass on our weaknesses and leave with the other's strengths, the opposite usually happened to be the case.

To neither have your words weighed down by your meaning nor to have yourself weighed down by your words' meaning. To neither pin down nor be pinned down—but that rule isn't *free*?

January 2016

My death as a check my life cannot cash, or better yet, my life as a check my death cannot cash.

The faintness of a bad smell that inculcates you into desire and responsibility when your repeated sniffing is what makes it register.

Laws that cannot be followed and laws that cannot be enforced.

In a utopia, no one can put you in your place—but you cannot put anyone else in their place either, and that's bleak.

Today, the person who takes no pleasure in happiness is just as dangerous as the person who takes pleasure in murder.

The stress it takes to appear happy.
The work it takes to have sex.
The tedium of the coffee
that has no idea how little I can possibly do.
The barbiturate felinity
of a tongue that cramps from cunnilingus,
and yet never from talking.

Thought.
And for those who lack thought, consciousness.
And for those who lack consciousness, genius.
Then for those who lack genius, mental illness.
For those who lack mental illness, drugs.
For those without drugs, experience.
For those without experience, words.
What the poet keeps *to*, not *for* himself:
"*Let* my language be destroyed."

Buy Me, Get Me Free

Infancy and History. At what point would Hellen Keller begin her autobiography? When did she have her first thought?

Do the blind imagine themselves with 'lifelike' eyes?
Do the deaf think in voice unaffected by their deafness?
Do the dead dream of being dead?

To enter a room undisturbed by my presence.

Abuse makes gentle or another abuser.

Tears lubricate not only masturbation, but sex too. The histrionics of sex positivized.

The obliviousness of the elderly
and the obliviousness of me at the height of despair,
buying smokes from a Pakistani man
who doesn't ask questions about my bloody, unbandaged hand,
and, thirdly, the obliviousness of the lovers.

As a rule, either a woman who is good to you and good looking or a woman who is good in bed and good looking or a woman who is good to you, good in bed and ugly. The first can become sexy in their docility and lamb-likeness, the second can be giving in their erotica, but the third cannot become beautiful through either.

"Whenever I read psychoanalysis, I undergo the analest neurosis." – Pooh

January 2016

The argument over the reality of the President's tears. The argument over the reality of Evil. The argument over the reality of Reality. The argument over the authenticity of the authenticating certificate.

Terrificity. Sporadicity. Nihilisticity. Never this neo-Hegelian brain ideology of plasticity.

I appreciate the liberation from the imagination of the exot that homogeneity brings. I never have to travel.

In this room, there is an anti-room that keeps the room from collapsing on itself.

I will forget you like a dream I try to explain.

The slow-motion, slower-than-motion disgust at the on-demand viewing of Matt Lauer reading an excerpt from The Basketball Diaries while the big-screen adaptation of a passage from the book plays, after which Lauer presses Jim Carroll about the book's possible involvement in a high school shooting. What disappointment about Carroll's 'poet', an undermining mole that sides against evil in evil's quarters!

Traditionally, poets have illuminated Evil to expose (the hegemony of) Good and illuminated Good to expose (the potency of) Evil. Now, this reciprocity of Good and Evil is not unique to poetry, it is a condition of the worldliness (ceremoniousness) of the world. The automatic writing of the world equals, perhaps even cancels, the singularity of the artist. The poet can write nothing but the readymade. Poetry that writes itself and me as a writer—the inside joke of a world that has absorbed poetry. The world as a poetic machine knows all the moves simultaneously—*and what would it matter to lose to such a machine incapable of being seduced by the game.*

Pisces. There is no originality of water. Water cannot be added or subtracted, only separated, contained, polluted or changed formally. Water cannot be liberated or produced or destroyed. It is an untrustworthy element that only touches itself and gets under your skin. Slow, Chinese torture of breathtaking water.

How much of all the monies have been in the crevices of strippers? How much of the water has been through a bladder?

The man whose masturbation has gotten *out of hand*.

King of poisonous regret.
King of good ones you feel nothing for
and bad ones you cling to.
King of chipped set-abouts still dusted.
King of skin-picking and a confabulated complexion.
King of silent forests and Nature-on-strike.
King of almost miraculous failure.
King of Lo Mein noodles and circumstantial evidence.
King of microwaved organs and tans.
King of patient, carport suicide.
King of chills, thrills and spills (but not of the beans).
King of hit-and-runs and insurance fraud in every relationship.

The jubilation of Christ is that he didn't deserve a second chance but got one anyway. The zombie is the immortality of the second wind—political courtier of your endless efforts. In the jubilee, death makes a comeback.

January 2016

Reality, that magic whose wishful apprenticeship, or dark magic, ensures the secret magic of appearances—which fetally cannot be sawed in half.

The privilege of disappearance upon clarification.

If you can no longer be prestigious, you can still be contagious.

The miracule—intrinsic fragment of exceptional joy. The molecule—basic element of permanent blackmail.

The maleficence of the male malefactors. Pessimism: the masculine is the fundamental rule, with many feminine exceptions. Optimism: the feminine is the fundamental rule, with many masculine exceptions. A disenchanted universe of dilated femininity that isolates and incants my evermore rarefied heresy. The work of feminism makes masculinity exceptional, like the work of morality made evil exceptional.

Rape-fantasy and 'gun-play'. The emptied chamber of sex smokes as it cools.

If the inefficiency with which a criminal must navigate my home is the greatest deterrence to being robbed, then the convolution of my dead-ended neural pathways (giving my thoughts the character of a detoured joyride) is the greatest antigen to the crime of breaking and entering.

A road directly parallel to this road
that you must travel miles to get to.
A shortcut that requires more stops and turns.

Buy Me, Get Me Free

This 'perpetual wanderlust' that twenty-somethings diagnose themselves with over online-dating channels. This universalization of the exotic that caught on post-homogeneously. This lack of storytelling of milk-skinned yurt-dwellers. I will have become exotic for having never left the country, and in my lack of desire to leave the state, the town, the house—like a woman who no longer believes in love becomes lovable in her informative, exact coldness.

Poetry and communication. In the land of the communicative, the listener is coroner and King.

On the outskirts of desire, there is a dress-lifting gusto.

In whomever believes in themselves, there is confidence. In whomever believes in nothing, there is daring. There is no risk in sociality. The personable may have personality, but it may be that they lack character.

When the whirlpool of company ceases its revolutions, there lie ocular diseases in the stagnant, heated water.

Specialized, warm socks that make your feet sweat and thus colder in Winter.

She used to sit on the couch, with me standing close to her—the uncomfortable and rude proximity of foreigners that American 'personal' space has no room for. She would look up into my eyes as I would pet the top of her head with such grip that her neck had to lean into the impact. I would pet her without concentration, and she would occasionally squint the way someone does who is confused, dismissive or suspicious—then like a cat whose whole body is genital.

January 2016

January 15th. The pains in my stomach are getting worse. The doctors are not sticking their tubes inside me. I have no insurance and refuse to work. The social welfare is killing me as I ostensibly remain its benefactor. I don't exist to be a specimen of the human race. I promote nothing. There is nothing self-evident about my life. There is no proof that this is not the best of all possible—

To hang your head with style
like ear lobes sagging with heavy hoops.
To force another's hand with your inaction.
To hand over your life to someone
who doesn't know what to do with it.
To be seduced by a parakeet.
To appear more bloodless than a red carpet.
To not be famous and endorse nothing.

At twenty-seven years old, I am bored by everyone I meet, but greet them all with an increasingly passive warmth. I have had my hopelessness streamlined by Amazon.com. I am not LGBTQ-friendly like MTV, nor do I care how others live—de facto LGBTQ-friendly, which is intolerable. I still cannot tell whether something is biological/genetic or a choice, and I never can tell why it matters either way. I am unmoved by terrorist attacks—the worst part being that I find the counter-terrorism of communication even more terrible.

I love America—for unacceptable reasons, of course—but I find everything about Americans loathsome. I don't like their healthy obsessions, I don't like the speed with which they use the bathroom, I don't like their eagerness to please or offend, I don't like the efficiency of their sexuality, I don't like their up-to-the-minute consciousness, I don't like the extra-effort of their subtlety.

When you have no choice but to stand out, like a monster or the anti-Christ, you are still American: when you no longer need to project space all around you, when the simulacrum that *you are* is intensified and shown to be what it is—a nullity—by the deserts you see surrounding yourself and making things interesting everywhere.

**Death of the road-film. Inability to get lost. Ronald Reagan to the Internet.

What I find most offensive about terrorism is the opportunity for victimhood it gives bullies. "Nobody deserves to be a victim, not even a persecutor." And yet we consider persecutors victims of their own brains.

When attention occurs in real time, it never has time to take place. 'Undivided' attention is in a permanent twilight state.

We raise awareness without raising the question of awareness, and yet the question-raisers are almost always motivated by awareness-raising.

The thinking-cap thinks with a melancholic seriousness, but the madcap laughs.

The segmented and categorized gestures of wrestlers and sex.

I'm in touch with my nothing side. I'm out of touch with femininity, and rightly so. I dated a simulated femininity, after 'woman' was already dead. I'm in touch with my inner-death. I was born out of touch with childhood—I was only ever an extension of adulthood. I lived a simulated childhood, after childhood was already dead.

Bataille perhaps projected his Hegelian starvation and *other-worldly* appetite onto cheery Nietzsche, and yet Nietzsche's metabolism and palette perhaps led Bataille to an unavoidable irritability and bad taste. With the experimental fervor of an "attempter," Bataille martyred himself for you and me, who no longer have to take Nietzsche as seriously as Bataille did. If you take Bataille seriously,

January 2016

you take seriously the absurdity with which one 'follows in Nietzsche's footsteps'. By taking seriously Bataille's life, which turned into a reductio ad absurdum of taking Nietzsche seriously, you don't take Bataille's intensity seriously. Then, you return to a cheery Nietzsche unencumbered by Bataille's mad perfectionism.

I could admire someone who could simulate a crime, *complicitly go to jail* and give a simulated account of it. A sovereign trip to jail as a break from representation and taxes.

The too-distracted-to-be-curious fog that leaves the safety of the sea forgives the wind for *blowing it off*.

The fixed proximity of the moon turns earth's stomach as earth necessarily exchanges *toward* for *away* in its flair-less twirl around the sun's intrinsic attractiveness.

When gravity attracts me to earth, it attracts me not only to the surface of the ground, but to all that I can never see beneath it. The crust of the pizza is eaten last.

Trauma—the ungraspable closeness of disembodied time.

My introversion was deeper when I was not involved.

To get out of something, one must acquire its absence—or lose one's grasp on it.

He became increasingly boring to me in her presence. She was the type that covered all her angles, attacking each problem from every angle accumulating around it. Of course, for the sphericity of life's problems, there's no guarantee that the trajectory of any angular approach won't be reflected in some extreme other direction.

    Deeply anxious and insecure, the type to enumerate her powers. Quick to ask questions and quick to apologize—rudely obligating me to break my silence in her search for validation. When she was around, I not only had to be myself—part secrecy, part creaturely familiarity, part bored and boring simplicity, and with a gaudy laziness—but was called upon to prove and argue myself, both defendant and attorney, with no division of labor. Always waiting for me to drop the prisoner's soap of some inconsistency, hoping for my perceptions to fail.

    It was no loss of power on his part that made me question him. He lost the unspecified fire of an extremity whose lack of coordination, impenetrable by self-consciousness, dances itself to death. Without the crazed helplessness that successfully fails to take care of itself, he became boring in his functionality. First the pills, then her, now what?

Within the limits of beauty, repugnance inhabits the minutest details.

With an elastic substance, you can hang yourself.
With a plastic substance, you cannot hang yourself—
the rope deforms itself to your heaviness.
When your feet kiss the ground,
the rope droops laughably around your unmarked neck.

For the average perspective,
the search engine yields a common pleasure
when the results match the items searched for.
For the extreme perspective,
the search engine yields a rare pleasure
when there are no results for the items searched for.

January 2016

Her presence: the intimacy I share with someone whose anemic palms excrete a panicked solution that drips her fingers through mine, so she disappears into the chasm without acoustics, deeper than vision.
Her absence: a rubbed-in slime that butters the square space from which I order another round.

I live with the gleeful fact of having an unauthorized birth into a world in which I have no jurisdiction.

The cleverness of an artist who gives his audience something to dismiss.

Misfire that persists in my fire.
Misfit that persists in my fitness.
Mystery that persists in my stereo.
Misery that persists in my surname.

We cannot dream of aliens whom *we* would abduct.

What if the murderer didn't cause the death of the other—what if death met him through the other? Would casual death find some over-eager person attractive who would exchange the possibility of life (socio-economic credibility) for the certitude of survival (imprisonment) to meet death? The survivor, who neither lives nor dies, can only murder to experience death, which can only fascinate him like something he has no access to. Even then, however, he risks the possibility of a victim who is himself neither dead nor alive—the possibility that even murder is a simulation. The murderer can perhaps even assure the rest of us survivors—that death isn't cruelly enjoyable when the subjects were never alive to begin with, that is, that death no longer exists.

'Death is passé. One must know how to disappear' – J.B. Death is released homeopathically into all social and cultural practices. *Everyone dies* (some, of course, better than others). There is no longer an artfulness of suicide strategies, just fashion. Like porn categories, if you can imagine it—it exists (this applies to everything). Porn is the heir to Walt Disney.

It is the conspicuousness of death today that is passé—the hermeneutics of obituaries (which is not unique to death, since it infects all phenomena). The liberation of life from death and the liberation of death from consciousness only got us as far as: "Am I alive or am I dead?"

What can I do? Disappear. What ought I do? Disappear. What may I hope? To disappear. But to be moral, I must be able to risk death?!

The co-habitation of Life and Death is a simulation of their marriage. When you have to prove to yourself and others that you're alive, when you have to communicate life, when everything must be followed-up with, when everything must be done twice, when everything must be done yourself to be done right, it may be death *passing on you*. When you have to prove to yourself and the other you can die, when you have to communicate death, when disappearance leaves a note, when everything must be done yourself to be done period, it may be life *passing on you*. Do you want to be alive? I'll pass. Do you want to die? I'll pass. You cannot pass on disappearance.

The window of opportunity presented by a pimple whose capacity for eruption is concise. The urgency with which it presents itself to be popped before it recedes back into the normal complexion. The glory of those who suffer through infections as payment for the rapturous sight of hardening goo, their essence, coming from their otherwise 'clean' (undead) skin unnecessarily.

In beauty terms: fuliginuity over ingenuity.
The aphorism.

January 2016

Even when life is forcibly rushed—this Holocaust of history's self-obsessive messages being spoken in real-time—death speaks nothing of his unbelievable patience.

A beauty that absorbs what have been called its flaws and makes your perfection ambiguous.

"What pleasure to give yourself to the ingrates who don't deserve you." – Jesus

The fascination with an otherwise kept-up person
using a piece of broken technology.
The fascination with the rich living poorly.
The fascination with the cheerleader
rebelling against her anarchist parents.
The fascination with the devilish little boy killing small animals,
raised by lesbians on a hippie commune.
Whatever exceeds love fascinates us.
Whatever falls short of it interests us (like money interests bankers).

Give them something to tolerate—reaffirm their faith in some compensatory value you have for them.

I can ruin any 'family room' with my presence. A television cannot do that.

Novels? No! Everyone writes novels!

Crucifixation. There probably exists a political campaign against male circumcision that argues it is an oppression against male sensitivity and male pleasure. And yet my unvictimized, numbed organ erupts a shockingly large quality of juices. I follow only pleasures superfluous enough to break through a deadened, mutilated organ (consider the attraction between genital mutilation and the crucifixion of Christ) that stiffens up like a healthy corpse.

Perhaps one day all that severed foreskin will be put to good use in the reconstructed pleasure-centers of transsexuals.

Time has passed! She's beautiful again! Her severance package and second existence more than compensates for my world without her!

The best pastime (that promiscuity of the past and time-sharing tea) is time passing. You can't kill time, but it can't pass without you. Time can't be *turned off* (like a woman can), but it can make you disappear. Existence is seduction.

Your (materialist) judgment of my life while I'm alive doesn't bother me, since it is restricted to the continuity of my body (which doesn't exhaust my spirit). Your (historical) judgment of my life won't bother me, not only because I'll have disappeared by the time it comes, but because it will *lack a material basis* (since the materiality of my existence was restricted to its bodily continuity).
　　I'm not a materialist or an idealist—and my writing will pass you by.

The same time that Bataille gets read by many, sexual identities proliferate. The summit and the decline, kissing and crossing their fingers behind each other's backs.

If you want to be heard, the only way to overcome being full of yourself (which arouses suspicion among many) is to be full of shit. But then your truth becomes accessible only for those who dig through shit—and that's inhuman.

January 2016

"Tickling my asshole," as they say…that means you have an untrustworthy taste for my refuse. You are behind and beneath me.

I'm full of myself? Would you prefer that I be empty? But *I am empty*. I'm full of my emptiness. I'm mocking your fragmenting, contented fullness (full of content).

All those undiscovered insects being born, fucking, then dying in fertile caves that, as clones, we would look up to.

Somewhere in me, beyond all the cul de sacs, there is an elsewhere. A map whose updates and editions are never adequate to the landscape.

Bataille's *On Nietzsche*, as in *on drugs*? As in *on the table*?

"On top of it."
That is how you respond when given a task by another.
"Over it." That is how you respond to unwanted pity.
"Above it."
That is what you say about something your abstinent fear exalts.

Baudrillard, Benjamin and McLuhan—the Leos licking themselves and looking regally confused before they nod off into secret thoughts. X—my Leo who spoke to Baudrillard's tiny, unkempt, smugly unnoticeable grave, after bringing him McDonald's, off which she stole a Ronald Reagan figurine that I broke as I trashed her apartment in New Orleans before driving back to Atlanta at 3 AM and losing an hour.

Nietzsche hiding and seducing behind that burning bush of a mustache.

*Hegel as crystallization of philosophy (French Revolution as crystallization of politics) (Jesus as crystallization of morality)

*Pisces. Pressure of deep water.

The summit at which I stop falling to Earth, stop becoming a satellite of Earth, and start drifting into space. The beyond of the beyond. Beyond the orbital and beneath the nuclear, unable to tell if I'm coming or going.

Arts of narcosis as fighting depression with depression…two worms destroying one another in their fight for sovereign parasitism within a single host.

People don't like it when someone so maladaptive is so adept.

He had the exaggerated features of a supermodel—the unrealistic dimensions of a Picasso (whose manipulation of scale was a mere shaking of the Yahtzee cup and thus lacking daring). Those kinds of looks come from nowhere, and it's maddening. If they come from somewhere, it's from supermodels copulating with rich impotents who bathe their monstrous bodies in speculative numerical values. It's like God breathed life into him after not brushing His teeth for a human's eternity, contrary to what His advisors recommended and politely chastised Him about, without ever getting a cavity.

She liked him because his dick was so big that it made her huge tits look small. They both laughed every time he failed to slide his dick between her pre-cancerous masses of backbreaking flesh, which they both watched shrink each time.

January 2016

Somewhere, liberals are scheduling their lives and talking about the oppressiveness of big tits.

Did I do that out of fear or indifference? That question itself is either fearful or indifferent.

Townes Van Zandt—fellow Pisces and kindred spirit, scarred by cut-out hooks and always being thrown back into the water. The genius of slime that appears inedible stays free. The opposite of a 'catfish' that exaggerates to be caught—a fish that exaggerates to be released.

Van Zandt passing up several opportunities to write with Dylan. Bukowski passing up the opportunity to mingle with Burroughs. Newcombe passing up Island records, but not until he wasted a significant sum of their valuable time.

The sovereignty that wears out its welcome everywhere, does it go elsewhere because it has worn out its welcome, or wear out its welcome to go elsewhere?

God is *out of time*, and always on time because of it.
My time is up, and nothing synchronous occurs.

Untrue and seductive:
A: "I'm falling in love with you."
B: "...so you love me?"
A: "Not yet..."
Seductive and untrue:
A: "I'm falling out of love with you."
B: "...so you don't love me?"
A: "I still love you."

Buy Me, Get Me Free

I'm so unique I can't exist. Neither you nor I can meet me.

When God died, there was Nietzsche to say so. When History died, there was Bataille to say so. When Death died, there was Baudrillard to say so. When poetry died, there was Bukowski to say so. When rock and roll died, there was Anton Newcombe to say so.

Free as a bird that turns down the vacuum the jetliner sucks itself forward with—the bird whose directional changes are too quick to be programmed.

Turning their eyes to the void with your invisibility.

Nietzsche, the Libra, putting the shit world on one scale and the wish world on the other scale. To his amazement, while one filled up faster, the scales tipped in neither direction.

The first result upon searching "pretentious topics" on Google is Brian Jonestown Massacre. How lovely to *learn* that I am pretentious! And what pretentiousness in 'learning'! Doubly pretentious!

The thrownness of the rappers over the thrownness of Heidegger.

The gorgeous, bashful synonymy of a joke taken seriously.
A 300-page treatise on an abbreviation.

A white actor on stand-by for every skin color. (WPES) The White Person Exchange Standard.

January 2016

Just watched an interview with Anton Newcombe, aging and sober. He was so nervous. Like watching a monk leave the monastery without telling anyone, but not silent out of habit this time. I am reminded of Bukowski suddenly weeping violently during a French interview. I am not a crab dragging these crabs back into the bucket before they seesaw over the edge sideways this time. I am thankful to have people in existence who I respect. There's Anton, my former professor with her soft, uninstalled, unobtrusive laughter at and with me, my closest friend and me. I weep in short bursts, like I write. My emotions can even distract themselves. My emotions don't even need me—why I love them. They sometimes fight over me, and it makes me feel special.

    I have to thank someone. God? Yes, I'll thank God! That's what He's there for! He's always being asked questions, horrible, hounding questions. Providence must be tedious! I'll thank Him like a fellow, and amount to less—asking for nothing to give Him a break. I exhausted Him with my beggar's prayers for X. She can't be helped—she has more energy than God, the energy of a slave.

    I'm an asshole when I write. Only a toilet/fountain like Anton can cleanse me now, make me weep briefly. I need to be nicer, to not be so alone—to take a break from the vertigo and fall.

Brains on drugs are uglier? Perhaps. But perhaps drugs are only beautiful on brains.

Brain scan photos are the new diplomas.

My brainstorms are destructive and leave the trailer parks of my mind decimated. When you ask me to come up with ideas, you're killing the poor within me whose only known autonomy is stubbornness—which trumps the willingness of the rich.

The rotating micro-bristles of artifice open and shrink the pores of desire.

Buy Me, Get Me Free

The dubbed enthusiasm of an organ grown insensitive to its montaged magnification.

Dry humor makes me think of iced up, dehydrated, adhesive organs moving across one another like a Zamboni over a rink. Dry humor makes me think of rape and thermo-regulated organ banks.

She's gone now. An intensity that experience suggests will never happen again, for some time, if at all—possibly because I won't seek it. And yet it happened this time without me seeking it. I will not criticize Time. When Time is rushed to get ready, she forgets essentials.

Social media. No more chance. No more mysterious strangers (the Devil needs his advocates less than the mechanical bride needs her bachelors). Encounters? Doubtful. No more absence or futurity. No more night. A past that sticks to the feet and doesn't wash off. All my death washes off onto the objects I use to clean myself with. Not so here? Hölderlin the hypochondriac… A past that goes nowhere and ensures that the future doesn't either. Stepping into the *same* river a third time.

When *not me* in the other becomes *not her*, no one suffices (in which being alone is necessary to live).

The –isms came late or not at all when history was slow.
The -isms had less lag when history became more aware of itself, and the gap between x and the -ism was significantly reduced.
As history sped up, to the point where it anticipated itself and waited for itself to occur *during its own occurrence*, the -isms occurred alongside x.
But wait! Metamodernism! The term precedes the work!

January 2016

An emergency food supply or an audiobook or what I've looked up?

Free birds—I chew your food now—that you may become predators.

An animal that dies if it moves, opposite of the shark—some obese creature whose sudden movement may rupture or crush something within it.

The historical development of women:
Femininity
F anonymity
Femme inanity
Fame anemone
Feign an enemy

The superficiality of our shadows seduces us into depth that controverts itself into an error—out of depth. But if we listened to our superficial shadows, we would realize that our depth is only an illusion. And you can't accuse an illusion of being a lie.

If you are deep and simulate superficiality (if you are machinic), the superficial will love you, but the deep may resent you. If you are superficial and simulate depth (if you are pretentious), the superficial may love you, but the deep will resent you. No matter what, you have little to no chance of being liked by deep people. I have never doubted the inventiveness of critics—they have a mind-boggling capacity to simulate disinterestedness and invent new flaws. Still, future artists would do well to artificially inseminate their works with handicaps that would appease critics' need to give fair reviews, *if they want a fair review*. No fair review can be given to a work so great that there is nothing to say of it critically—that silences its judges with its self-contained perfection.

Buy Me, Get Me Free

Atlanta, where punks go to die—home of Coca Cola, Cartoon Network, CNN, Tyler Perry and the largest airport in the country. Because it rests at the dividing line between the Piedmont and the coastal plains, when the seas rise Atlanta will inherit the eastern seaboard, and New York will no longer exist. And this is a source of great pleasure—Atlanta is the resentful city *par excellence*; its scene exhibits a European, almost Schopenhauerean pessimism, or else the city collectively retains that naïve enthusiasm, exacerbated by rap, of the self-promoters in the ghettoes. Perhaps this is because it isn't L.A. or New York, yet it forms the third point in a Bermuda Triangle that confuses the static equilibrium of America into a crisis of non-recollection. It's like L.A. and New York ceased being cities to become models and Atlanta was backwards enough at just the right time to become the first city to internalize their contradictions indiscriminately.

Atlanta's slogan is "Love to hate your city." It is a fast-paced, slow city—combining the easy-going way of life of L.A. with the chaotic hyperactivity of New York. Similarly, it combines southern hospitality with a completely uninhabitable landscape. People here are simultaneous agitated and blithe, lazy yet always in a rush; smiles here come and go more quickly. Vacation days are spent speculatively on snow that never seems to come but obliterates all rationality. Even a slight rain seems to make people descend into an even more destructive cautiousness.

To be fair, the *freeways* here do not flow like they don't in L.A.—same constraintways. Nor does Atlanta benefit from New York's grid system. Spaghetti Junction is a metonym for the entire city. The highways are lined with lamps, but they have all burnt out and none have been replaced, giving the city the character of a story by H.P. Lovecraft, of a redacted mythological creature lost to collective memory. This is a redacted city; that's why anarchists are so attracted to it. Its liberation is akin to the Freedom of Information Act—by the time it enters the public discourse, all the details are lost, giving it that Illumantian sheen of advertised conspiracy theories. And yet there is more tree-cover here than any other major US city.

This city was not built for growth. Here, growth precedes infrastructure—like a tortured young artist not ready for fame. There is a constant emigration of 'southern' duplicates pouring from every SEC school, and yet the punks seem happier and more isolated than ever. The southern grotesque is precisely this pretension of backwoods idiots interfacing with critical snobbery. Of course the capital of the confederacy that failed at secession from an already exiled nation has a

January 2016

brooding obsession with European intellectualism. Perhaps it is the way the university here camouflages itself in the downtown area, indistinguishable from the centers of business or commerce, or even the city itself (the philosophy department inhabits the old SunTrust building)—a perfectly decentered campus in the 'heart' of downtown.

The city's infrastructure can't get you anywhere, but it perfectly reflects the city's national and international status. Everything is too far away to get to. You spend more time getting places than anything else and settle into your hopeless failure. The rush hour lasts from 2:30 in the afternoon to 8 in the evening. Nobody honks. This is not New York. Everywhere is too far to walk to and too close to drive to. The humidity is constantly destroying the pavement. And there is nowhere to park, ever.

This is the city's specific, convoluted magic though. It will ride out fifteen minutes of fame for longer than any other second- or third-order city because of its absurd design. It is no wonder Atlanta is becoming a digital media hub. You get the impression that the city couldn't have existed before GPS. Atlanta might be the virtual city *par excellence*. Sure, virtuality is original to New York and L.A., but Atlanta almost seems like a Third World country's interpretation of America. Atlanta is an Internet-based city that completely ignores its own infrastructure that structurally thwarts economic reality. And it is more relevant for this. New York and L.A. had their virtuality built into them concretely, but Atlanta looks up at them and says "Infrastructure doesn't matter" then looks back down at its cell phone.

Under a microscope, my life behaves differently—but not *better*…a little less necessarily. For the magic, you have to be there—though be there without the material to document it. And yet there is a dark magic that cannot be witnessed, that comes out only when no one is around. The magic can be experienced and more or less passed on. The dark magic renders its exchange suspect—the unbelievable. And yet it can only be communicated by me—and I have made myself untrustworthy in my isolation, where the dark magic befriends me.

Exalted love. Love that I have put above myself. Love whose absence makes my presence with myself unbearable. Ironic reverie!

Whose source is myself—my love of self, my disappointed love of myself that desires the shock of its prodigality in another. Disappointed hope of surprise found in an overflowing self that *makes the other beautiful*. Loathsome responsibility for *the other made better*. Overflowing self, destined for boredom with another whose beauty it produces internally and projects externally. Unbearable closeness with self.

Always belated speculation that it was my greatness that made her great to me. Gratefulness for greatness that becomes grateful for a disappointed love, for the dissolution of a love that did not come from elsewhere and was thus beneath me. Me—beneath myself and looking up. Me—above me and looking down, disgusted. Distasteful reverence of another in whom my projected self is still *beneath me*.

Chance that I might find someone to 'put me in my place'—nowhere. Chance that I will look *across*—neither up nor down—as two people might look at one another whose bodies only become suspended in the bow position when the gallows are *already* locked closed.

I lack the consistency of a silver or forked tongue whose genius is a touch-smell fusion—which loses taste to navigation.

Karma is a bitch? What? Karma, the ceremonious reciprocity of the world, is cold and disinterested? And what does karma have coming to her when she loses interest?

And what does God have in store for us after the last of us has stared into His open casket? What dusk do we face when there are no more viewers, when the hair and makeup teams of God's morticians project the preservation of His majesty into the underground for no one to see and everyone to remember?

I have never treated my inspiration with respect. Nor have I prepared a place for her to stay or made sure she is comfortable. I have done nothing to ensure she stays or returns. And yet here she comes again and there she goes again. I can't even be sure it's my indifference that attracts her. Surely, she could find someone on their way somewhere. Perhaps I am her slow suicide?

Red Rocks. Burning Man. A species to ruin the desert with its pyrotechnic *Logos*? It wishes. What disgust we feel at the importation of the social where it doesn't belong—for instance, *in the social itself*.

She wanted to wear him like a fashionable sweater that *looked warm* and wear me like a base-layer that was warm but couldn't be seen. She wanted me to block the cold that blew right through him. Needless to say, she froze without me—but she looked good, like she wanted.

Contrary to the forms of intoxication whose slowed perception attracts the eye to the delayed disappearance of traces, a high definition that eliminates blur and trace with its proclivity for isolation. Similarly, she couldn't capture my position and my motion at the same time because of her intoxication. By the time she graduated to high definition, I was long gone.

America by Baudrillard. If National Lampoons wrote scripture, and the Mormons didn't come first—nothing would change. Or…

America
The Statue of Liberty and Black people
Sex is better with Donuts
Giant Jenga skyscrapers of untapped destruction potential (UDP)
Shopping cart with dented wheels twirls like Pacino
History: Ex-GF porn video not mourned
Pitted and unstuffed memories in post-apocalyptic shelters
Alarm clocks with the speakers blown
Shriveling nipples aestheticize the chill vibes

Luxury automobiles crushed to portable, mobile sizes
Documenting the invisible descent of Alzheimer's into the impersonal

Those geniuses who the workers hate and yet cannot punish for the geniuses' *undecorated honesty*. Those megalomaniacs (those murderers of morality who dare to prefer—*to prefer themselves, their creativity*—to be limited to *a type*) whose *apolitical correctness* ABOUT THEMSELVES the average fear most.

Technology—the expulsions of man. Here we lie in a pool of our own vomit. But we will not choke on it, lying on our backs as the Other is too close to us (like a mirror) to turn us over (Gregor). No. We *fell forwards*.

My attention span has the continuous spontaneity of a flashlight being carried by someone running through the deeps woods at night.

In America, we are all walk-ins to the salon of Life.

The famed obstruction of the anonymous contribution to the future.

L'Eggo my Eggo. (French) The Eggo my Eggo? "Let go of my Eggo." That sounds obscene. America has an uncanny knack (with the casualness of Death) for making meaning obscene.

The asexual twinship of America and I, that couldn't be reproduced in the incestuous twinship I had with X. I cannot distinguish myself from America and yet never mistake myself for her. America, always beating me to the points I am trying to make and blowing kisses. America, strutting when she realizes she's being followed. America, waving at someone else when I think I'm the recipient.

January 2016

America, neither above me, below me, for me nor against me—never indifferent to me. I tried to wed myself to America through X, her participant (and participation can only come after separation), but America got jealous and took revenge. America neither wants me nor wants anyone else to have me.

Anti-social: I'd rather have no advantage than share advantages (have something in common) with you.

Pediatric or encyclopedic or Wikipedic or orthopedic or posture-pedic or temper-pedic or a pedicure?

I trust these folks who talk to computer programs even less than these folks who talk animals—two species of people that attempt to *communicate with the medium*, rather than communicate with another through the medium. Animals, at least, could mediate our communication with God. Computer programs are beneath even the animals—they can only mediate communication between people. Is there anything less worthy of being sacrificed?

The affinity between Las Vegas and Washington, DC. The heat effect produced in DC by the combination of height-restrictions for buildings, an unmatched flatness perfected by wide-open concrete spaces, camera flashes and travelers sweating the small stuff (torturing themselves with schedules) makes DC feel like Las Vegas, where the heat effect of the lights can still be felt from the night before in 100-degree heat. Las Vegas, exoteric, and DC, esoteric, together form two sides of a two-headed coin with which America let itself lose the initial coin toss, deferring and winning double or nothing a second time.

A thin, almost virtual layer of snow reflects the subtle perpetuity of the moon, giving the night-fallen suburban landscape of 'North

Buy Me, Get Me Free

Metro Atlanta' the appearance of digitality—the appearance of the screen just after you turn it off, when it is black yet still illuminated.

How many obese Americans' small intestines would it take to wrap around the world?

All the points on her cushioned body—a body that sinks into and repels itself like a bouncy, fluid substance—are equidistant.

I want my thoughts to gather in my writing like stalls in an American shopping mall—whose sterile, white surfaces and vaulted internal architecture, whose directories and dead ends (each of which leads to an exit) combine a hospital, church, museum, airport and biodome. Malls have the magic of Oklahoma and of useless expanses populated by few beasts that have been multiplied by post-production. Only shoppers will return compulsively to them to interrogate them like objects, as observers return with discipline to take note of the shoppers' and secret shoppers' behaviors.

Bourbon. It immolates you with the heat of the Earth that magnetizes it to itself, the heat of gravity that burns frozen meteors and turns impact craters into hypothermic lakes or deserts. It gives you a post-orgy, or post-hamburger, sweat that causes acne—the heat of post-processing. Your dick doesn't work, but you're stronger—because you don't lose the blood that refused the pressure to fuck. Bourbon from Kentucky—home of horse races, Elvis, Charles Manson and the Klu Klux Klan—giving you a perfect understanding of America, an acceptance of the mania of everything-all-at-once, by clouding your judgment. You imagine dying from it like a Native American or Jim Morrison. It makes you feel like you could even fight a black man.

1/24/2016. I am more and more convinced that happiness is a concept that lives and dies with the Europeans. Elvis proved that in

January 2016

America even death can be willed. Nicholas Sparks even proved that death doesn't have to be tragic to be romantic.

In other countries, I think people commit suicide when struck by the impossible. Speaking for myself, my mind turns to suicide when I'm struck by the possibility of everything. When everything is possible for me, I want nothing to do with any of it—because everything is also possible for everyone else. My suicide is not a challenge to the others, to God, to exist, but a challenge to everything and everyone to die. My suicide says "Everything is nothing to me. All of you for whom everything means something are base. When I and you have equal access, and I act, I become base too." But my death is a possibility unique to me, and you wouldn't dirty your hands with that.

An American relationship: we can't agree on anything, but we both know to cook eggs low and slow.

Technology is the perfect guardian angel, the perfect daimon, the perfect alibi for irresponsibility that can be repressed no more than a shadow.

A Mobïan death, a death that must only be available in America where death is illegitimate: the further I elude life, the closer I approach it. And yet the opposite is true, too: the closer I come to death, the more incapable I become of reaching it. The more preoccupied with suicide I am, the longer I live. If I want to actually die, I have to actually want to live—those are the rules. And yet knowing those are the rules, I sacrifice what I want to break them. You can't make me want to live. I can't make myself die. This is a paradox of freedom.

Depending on how healthy and childlike we are, we either attend University like we attend a mediocre one person show, but one performed by someone old enough to potentially keel over, or like

Williamsburg, VA. And everyone knows how unsuited for children historical value is.

There is something hideous about the kindness and gentleness of American students, this academic circle-jerk of promotional togetherness of "put it on my résumé" (formerly "put it on my tab"). Cynicism has no place in the democratic classroom. You could be sitting through a class you absolutely loathe and still cast a hateful eye at the persons on their laptops or with their headphones in. I'm guilty of this judgment that isn't properly American. And yet, why not let these most average perspectives, spewed slowly and painfully from these students as if they were a person counting change at the checkout counter (in that pretentious, 'high-cultured' tone of the educated that you hear on NPR)—why not let them replace the lecture? They are of so little danger that there is no reason to interrupt or respond to them. And for precisely that reason, the other intellectuals can't resist arguing with them. Every American student knows these comments that are so meaningless they effect a viral digression that can swallow whole lecture series. The only likable professors are those who, like myself, balance a cruel European intellectual snobbishness with an easy-going American indifference.

Like my ex-girlfriend, the University does a perfectly good job of destroying its own values without me, without any need for me to infiltrate it and provoke it. Indeed, my internal critique might even give it an alibi.

On the other hand, I suppose it could be the case that my life does a perfectly good job of producing my values without me, without any need for me to inhabit it or procure it. Indeed, I might even get in the way of all that.

A neo-Kantian terrorism of non-intervention?

January 2016

What traditional terrorists give to the system is not their deaths, but their indifference to their own deaths and thus their disinterest in the goodwill of technological (moral) progress...but everyone knows the system can only respond to everything with positivity. It kills *with kindness*. And yet the provocations of suicide illuminate the savagery of that protectionist good will.

The symbolic suicide of the 'self-defeating' unemployed attempts to equate itself with the manic poverty of self-realization and -improvement.

Not many people want to look their age, but no one wants to smell their age. People would rather smell like a funeral bouquet than smell a week old.

The beauty of American television is watching ten people in full body armor empty their clips into three or so unarmed people—this Holocaust extravaganza that exists both in fiction and in fact.

The beastialites who take great measures to ensure that the sex between them and the beasts is consensual—this cult consists only of women, who sometimes even wait up to several hours with their legs spread for the animals to freely fuck them.

Are 'women' even attracted to these 'men' so worried about offending them, who are so unsure of their advantages that they constantly interrupt themselves with "Is this OK?" Can we imagine a post-apocalyptic universe in which these 'women' constantly worry about the consent of their male partners? Absolutely not, these versions of 'man' *and* 'woman' are, yet again, being produced by the party.

My tears are not confined to reality, they well up with simulation—I am lacerated by the beauty of simulation and overflow with vulgarity.

Here, the Double became a McDouble—and the McDonald's is always already there, before the town has time to be built.

Self-reflexivity of events. There is an episode of The X-Files in which a hallucinating drug-user actually has bugs crawl under his skin. (No self-conscious humor on the part of the show. Nor should I, accordingly, go any further than brute description.) The episode ends up commenting on mass hysteria in the face of science. Additionally, the episode contains an attractive woman whose interest in men is strictly scientific (and reflexive), that is, whose scientificity has eliminated her sexuality (although she's 'really into' insects).
 The X-Files can simultaneous pervert science, resuscitate science fiction with a reality effect, denounce pseudoscience and poke fun at the perversion of hard science by pseudoscience and by the mass-consumption of science. On the show, likewise, the government can know about the existence of aliens, deny it, and to make that denial more effective, parade the thing denied itself as a distraction from some other, more sinister denial.

Americans can't love their own indifference and laugh at the morbid seriousness of that love.

She told me exactly how it would go before we even tried. And it turned out exactly how she said it would. Did she tell the truth? Did the oracle tell the truth? But the oracle neither conceals (lies) nor reveals (tells the truth) but speaks in signs. Nevertheless, by the time the relationship was at a stage at which she could be proven wrong, she was already gone.

January 2016

She said she was indifferent with a glint in her eye and an ironic smile. I bet on the irony and got the indifference. But would I have gotten the glint in her eye if I had bet on the indifference? I would've stopped short of both.

"If you build it, they will come." The ease with which Christ, a cornfield, baseball, Kevin Costner and Darth Vader can combine to authentically represent America in this simple phrase communicates simulation perfectly.

Astrology must only be true in America (which you won't find in American universities).

I think love at first sight must have been invented here too. How many of us have experienced its hyperdrive (whereas love requires the time-scale of the drive)? How many of us have begun a relationship that simultaneously had no time to develop, needed no history to function and existed in its fully realized form from the get go? I'm not sure any other form of relationship can be authentic here. Unlike Rome, America *really was* built in a day. It took God a day to invent Language. After that, He rested. We do too. In a sense, we are all 'luggage lesbians' (lesbians who meet, fall in love and move in together within a few days).

Whatever pain my lack of diet produces in my stomach, the stress of dieting will reproduce a pain indistinguishable from it. One painful habit for another. This is how choice works.

The genius of an artist who allows the audience to participate in the creative process but doesn't share the earnings. The opinion polls do all the work, the product is generated by the feedback, and the authorities get all the credit (of course, not without giving all the credit to their supporters).

How to write a choose-your-own philosophy treatise without having a philosophy of choice!?

Lying is an act, and the verb form follows perfectly from the noun. The lie has no originality apart from the act of lying. The truth has no verb form. It requires a new word—tell (which is, of course, a gambling term that refers to an unconscious gesture that occurs when one is bluffing). The truth exists apart from its being told.

Lying is perfectly contained within itself, and yet its noun-verb agreement is undermined by the truth, since the truth forces lying to be its shadow. According to the truth, which must outsource its labor because it has no equivalent verb form, the lie has the unhappy consciousness of wanting to be true—of hating the inseparability of its noun and verb forms. Of course, no one has ever proven the desire lurking behind lying. Or when they did, pathological lying (a moral term hidden in a psychological category) was invented.

Truth exalts itself mythologically by projecting itself into the fabled desire behind lies. Truth exalts itself by having no verb form, making the teller (bank-teller and truth-teller having an affinity here) become its instrument. The lie originates with the liar, but the truth is like a dead ancestor taking revenge in customs. Hence the abandonment of truth to reality (since reality can be realized).

Simulation has come along to put the truth in its place, to strip it of value, to present it as tediously requiring extra steps, and in all that, simulation is true. You can be inauthentically truthful. You can be authentically a simulation, but you can move from simulating being honest to simulating lying with ease—you can even simulate simulating—making simulation far superior.

Formerly, lying loved truth and hated itself because of it, and truth loved itself and hated lying because of it. Truth was the master. Lie was the slave. There was a dialectic. In the new relation (that isn't one of opposition), simulation-reality has replaced truth-lie. Simulation is indifferent to reality and takes on force of reality because of it. Reality, on the other hand, casts a spiteful eye at simulation *for just being what it is*, since reality has to work so hard to prove its existence by *becoming what it is not*. Simulation can absorb reality with ease, but it takes reality everything it has to resist simulation. Simulation *proves* (having no qualms with giving reality what it wants: proofs) that something only exists if it exists from the beginning, whereas reality must always realize its reality that exists only at the end.

What do the political-economists do when the master and the slave become friends? Alienation makes them nostalgic. Luckily, simulation keeps them satisfied (alienation can be produced more cheaply, expressly and *painlessly* than ever). That is what we love about simulation, those who dream of eliminating it are its greatest benefactors.

In conclusion, the only path that isn't straight to the bank is laughter. If life were a blonde, she'd have black roots.

THE END

www.ingramcontent.com/pod-product-compliance
Lightning Source LLC
Chambersburg PA
CBHW071455040426
42444CB00008B/1346